decentering
whiteness
in the
workplace

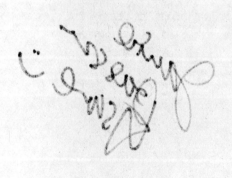

decentering whiteness in the workplace

A Guide for Equity and Inclusion

JANICE GASSAM ASARE, PhD

Berrett–Koehler Publishers, Inc.

Berrett-Koehler Publishers, Inc.
1333 Broadway, Suite 1000
Oakland, CA 94612-1921
Tel: (510) 817-2277
Fax: (510) 817-2278
www.bkconnection.com

ORDERING INFORMATION
Quantity sales. Special discounts are available on quantity purchases by corporations, associations, and others. For details, contact the "Special Sales Department" at the Berrett-Koehler address above.
Individual sales. Berrett-Koehler publications are available through most bookstores. They can also be ordered directly from Berrett-Koehler: Tel: (800) 929-2929; Fax: (802) 864-7626; www.bkconnection.com.
Orders for college textbook/course adoption use. Please contact Berrett-Koehler: Tel: (800) 929-2929; Fax: (802) 864-7626.

Distributed to the U.S. trade and internationally by Penguin Random House Publisher Services.

Berrett-Koehler and the BK logo are registered trademarks of Berrett-Koehler Publishers, Inc.

Printed in Canada

Berrett-Koehler books are printed on long-lasting acid-free paper. When it is available, we choose paper that has been manufactured by environmentally responsible processes. These may include using trees grown in sustainable forests, incorporating recycled paper, minimizing chlorine in bleaching, or recycling the energy produced at the paper mill.

Library of Congress Cataloging-in-Publication Data
Names: Asare, Janice Z. Gassam, author.
Title: Decentering whiteness in the workplace : a guide for equity and
   inclusion / Janice Gassam Asare, PhD.
Description: First edition. | Oakland, CA : Berrett-Koehler Publishers,
   [2023] | Includes bibliographical references and index.
Identifiers: LCCN 2023012858 (print) | LCCN 2023012859 (ebook) | ISBN
   9781523005550 (paperback ; alk. paper) | ISBN 9781523005567 (pdf) | ISBN
   9781523005574 (epub) | ISBN 9781523005581 (audio)
Subjects: LCSH: Racism in the workplace. | Discrimination in employment. |
   Diversity in the workplace. | Equality. | Corporate culture.
Classification: LCC HF5549.5.R23 A73 2023 (print) | LCC HF5549.5.R23
   (ebook) | DDC 658.30089—dc23/eng/20230317
LC record available at https://lccn.loc.gov/2023012858
LC ebook record available at https://lccn.loc.gov/2023012859

First Edition
31 30 29 28 27 26 25 24 23   10 9 8 7 6 5 4 3 2

Book producer and text designer: Happenstance Type-O-Rama
Cover designer: Daniel Tesser

*To the ancestors who paved
the way for us all today.*

●

*To those who are navigating workplaces
where you may feel you don't belong:*

●

*May this book provide the tools needed to
make our world a better place.*

contents

foreword

D r. Janice Gassam Asare and I first connected in early March of 2020. I was in the middle of my book tour for *Me and White Supremacy*. A global pandemic had not happened. And George Floyd was still alive and unknown to most of the world.

Three years later, our world looks so different.

We can all agree that 2020 was a year for the history books. We are forever changed by the losses we have suffered. But we are also changed by the ways that our voices were unleashed to call out white supremacy and anti-black racism.

One of the major issues that rose to center stage that year was the systemic racism and anti-blackness taking place in businesses around the world, and especially in the US. In fact, 2020 became the year that it was not only necessary, but normal, to talk about decentering whiteness.

But while many organizations shared their Instagram black squares and BLM statements that summer, it's clear that many did not carry that same energy past 2021.

That's why this book matters. Because we cannot go back to how things were.

As someone who has spent years writing and speaking about the importance of anti-racism, I believe this book is a powerful resource for anyone who is serious about creating truly equitable workplaces.

One of the biggest barriers to an anti-racist world is the tendency to center whiteness in all aspects of organizational culture. This book provides a direct and straightforward analysis of what this means and how it manifests in the workplace. Readers will gain a deep understanding of the different ways, from hiring practices to performance evaluations, that whiteness is centered at work and the importance of centering the most marginalized employees.

But this book is not just about analysis.

It also provides a guide on how to recognize and decenter whiteness within oneself and at work. It offers practical solutions for people to contribute individually and systemically to anti-oppression efforts. Whether you are a leader, a DEI (diversity, equity, and inclusion) practitioner, or simply someone who wants to be part of the solution, this is a crucial guidebook that will help you make a real difference.

As the need for racial equity in the workplace becomes ever more urgent, this book provides a timely and necessary roadmap for change. I encourage everyone who cares about creating a more just and equitable world to engage with this book and put its insights into action.

We must decenter whiteness in our workplaces, and our world, so that we can all have the privilege of living in the dignity of our full humanity.

—LAYLA F. SAAD, *New York Times* bestselling
author of *Me and White Supremacy*

introduction

What Is White-Centering?

Every spring, I attend the annual conference of a professional organization that I'm part of. Recently I was on the conference's planning committee and my role was to find speakers to facilitate a discussion on the remote work experiences of marginalized employees. Two speakers that I had found asked me to moderate their discussion, and I agreed. On the morning of their talk, we had about twenty people in attendance. When the speakers asked the audience what they'd seen as far as the experiences of marginalized employees in remote work settings, a few people raised their hands. One person, a Black woman, shared that her manager had asked her if her hair was real when she showed up one day with a new hairstyle on a Zoom call with colleagues. She explained that although the pandemic has slowed these types of microaggressions, they hadn't completely gone away.

I picked up the microphone and thanked her for sharing her experiences. I reiterated these sentiments, emphasizing that many of these subtle slights still continue in virtual settings. Afterward, the speakers told the audience we would stop for a ten-minute break and then reconvene. As I was gathering my belongings to make a water run, a woman came up to me, seeming eager to chat. She proceeded to say to me, "You know, that was an interesting story that was shared. I went through something similar." For the sake of the story, let's call her Karen. Intrigued, I asked Karen to elaborate. She explained that when she was young, her family frequently traveled to Mexico. Karen shared that her being a white person with red hair was shocking to the people in Mexico, and many of them asked her if they could touch her hair. She said, "Sometimes they didn't even ask. They just walked up to me and touched my hair!" Karen paused for my reaction. I looked at her with no words. I smiled and thanked Karen for sharing her story. She smiled back and I walked out of the room to a nearby water fountain. My mind was racing as I left, annoyed at how Karen centered herself and her experience, rather than considering the experience of racial microaggressions the Black woman shared earlier.

When we came back from the ten-minute break, the story that Karen had shared with me was still swirling around in my head. The moderators shifted the topic from marginalized experiences to allyship and advocacy. A white woman in the crowd, I'll call her Rebecca, raised her hand to ask a question: "How can we be more supportive of employees who have these experiences? How do we become more of an ally to marginalized employees?" The speakers nodded and then both proceeded to share their insights, providing some concrete actions regarding what allyship meant for them. After they both spoke, one of them asked me if I had anything I wanted to add. I nodded emphatically and they passed me the mic. "One of the barriers to allyship," I explained, "is a lack of compassionate listening. Sometimes aspiring 'allies' want to relate so badly to someone's experience even when it's an experience they know nothing about." I went on to share something that I heard *New York Times* bestselling author Ijeoma Oluo say in an Instagram video. Oluo explained that she had stopped doing public readings of her book *So You Want to Talk about Race*. When she would do such readings in the past, particularly the chapter where she talked about her experiences as a Black biracial woman with Afro-textured hair, she would get white women lining up afterward to talk to her. They would say how they knew how she felt. They, too, experienced hair discrimination. They would share that having curly hair or red hair made them feel ostracized or othered. Oluo explained that white people's attempts to "relate" often ended up invalidating the harm that racially marginalized people experience.

After summarizing what Oluo shared in that particular video post, I ended my response by saying, "Having curly hair or having red hair is not the same as having Afro-textured or Black hair. There are systems designed to oppress Black hair. There are laws made to oppress Black people's hair. To compare an individual experience of being treated differently to a structural issue that systemically harms a group of people is not a fair comparison."

I went on to tell a story about my mom. After my maternal grandmother passed away, someone had said to my mom, "I'm sorry for your loss. I know how you feel." That was infuriating to her. She would say to me, "They have no idea how I feel. Why would they say that?" The same way that trying to relate to someone who is grieving feels like a diminishment or invalidation of their feelings, when white people try to relate their unrelated experiences to the harm and terror that racially marginalized people experience, it causes further harm. It makes the person who opened up about their experience feel unheard.

After I shared my response to Rebecca's question about allyship and advocacy, I let the main speakers take the reins and close out their discussion by providing additional strategies for allyship in the workplace. When the discussion ended, I grabbed my phone and asked them if the three of us (the two speakers and me) could take pictures. I'm one of those annoying people that always wants to take pictures and videos before, during, and after an event. After all, if there are no pictures, did it really happen? The three of us were seated at a table at the front of the room and we walked to the projector where the first slide of the presentation was visible. I asked the first person I saw to take a photo of us. Coincidentally, that happened to be the redheaded woman who had shared her Mexico story with me. As I handed Karen my phone and before I could ask if she would take a photo, she muttered something under her breath, almost as if to ensure that no one would hear her. She said, "You know, I didn't appreciate that example you gave." Confused, I responded, "Huh?" Karen explained, "Right after I told you about my experience in Mexico, you used an example, basically calling me out." I paused. I was confused at where this was coming from. She and I had a personal one-on-one conversation that, to my knowledge, no one else had heard. When I was sharing Ijeoma Oluo's story during the larger discussion, I was sharing that with the entire audience of about twenty people to answer Rebecca's specific question. At no point while telling that story did I ever mention Karen or what she had told me. When there was a question that came up about allyship, I felt it was necessary to mention what allyship is *not*.

As I was explaining this to Karen, she interrupted me and said in a low, scolding, almost disciplinarian voice, "I did not like that *at all*." I laughed at this display of peak whiteness. Rather than trying to recognize why her statements were problematic, Karen had convinced herself that I was somehow trying to vilify her. One of the speakers walked closer, seeing the exchange take place. Slowly walking closer to me, she asked, "Janice, you good?" I muttered that everything was fine and then proceeded to ask Karen (whose real name I never actually got) if she could take our photo. She reluctantly obliged. After taking a few photos, I thanked her and she handed me my phone back. I looked through the pictures to make sure they were good and then walked away to gather my belongings. The speaker who had asked me if I was good walked up to me and asked what happened. She had overheard bits and pieces of our exchange. When I explained to her what happened, she just laughed and shook her head.

That experience was a classic example of white-centering, which occurs much more often than we even realize. That exchange, though seemingly minor, stayed with me. It reminded me of how, in any and every situation, as my good friend Joquina Reed often reminds me, "whiteness always seeks to center itself." In my second book, *The Pink Elephant*, I wrote about white-centering and defined it as "the act of a white person refocusing a conversation on themself when a BIPOC is sharing an experience. This often includes diverting a racial dialogue to discuss your feelings and emotions as a white person versus focusing on the feelings of BIPOC and what is being said." Since writing *The*

Pink Elephant, I believe this definition must be expanded because of the pervasive nature of white-centering and the insidious ways it shows up in our world. To expand the initial definition that I wrote, I would now define white-centering as

> *actions and behaviors that prioritize, uplift, amplify, and venerate white people and the dominant white culture above other cultures and communities.*

The Difference between White-Centering and White Supremacy

How is white-centering different from white supremacy? White-centering is one manifestation of white supremacy culture; it's one of the results of white supremacy. White supremacy, according to *Merriam-Webster* Online, is "the belief that the white race is inherently superior to other races and that white people should have control over people of other races," as well as "the social, economic, and political systems that collectively enable white people to maintain power over people of other races."[1] It is important to note that anyone, regardless of their racial background, can center whiteness, which we will talk about in more detail throughout this book. Based on these definitions, non-white people cannot be white supremacists in a society where they do not hold the power. Racially marginalized groups do not collectively have the ability to create social, economic, and political systems or uphold and maintain power over others. Racially marginalized communities *can*, however, spout talking points and engage in actions that contribute to the prioritization of white-dominant culture.

Why should white people care about decentering whiteness in the workplace? I understand that by asking this question I am centering whiteness. But I still felt like it was important to mention that white supremacy culture harms us all, including white people. I've written specifically about this before, in two of my articles for *Forbes*. White supremacy culture discourages imagination, encourages perfectionism and a scarcity mindset,[2] and is also harmful to the environment[3]—issues that affect us all. In the long term, white supremacy culture harms everyone on this planet, despite the fact that white people also benefit from this system in varying ways in the short term.

At an early age we all learn to center white feelings, white experiences, and white knowledge to the detriment of other racial groups. White-centering can be thought of as one result of white supremacy culture, but anyone can center whiteness because whiteness is not a person but a system. In this book, we will explore the many ways that we center whiteness in the workplace. In order to decenter whiteness in the workplace, first we must have an understanding of how it is centered. We'll examine how white-centering leads to the creation of workplace policies, practices, processes, and procedures—for example, who we hire and who we promote—that prioritize white people, particularly those that fit the model or prototype of whiteness. Lastly, we'll dive into other aspects of white-centering, including anti-blackness. Whiteness cannot exist without its opposite: blackness. We will examine the ways that anti-blackness shows up in the workplace. Throughout the book, I'll share strategies that you can implement to decenter whiteness in your workplace.

Decentering whiteness requires us to understand white-centering while also having the ability to recreate, redesign, and remove harmful systems that center whiteness. I welcome you on this journey to decentering whiteness both in your workplace and in your life. This book is for anyone that has struggled to create a workplace built on equity and inclusion. Equity will never be a reality while whiteness is being centered in our workplaces. Let this book be your guide to recognizing the ways that your workplace prioritizes whiteness and the ways *you've* prioritized whiteness in your own life. I will be sharing my own experiences of upholding and centering whiteness and the processes I actively engage in to decenter whiteness in my own life. Please understand that decentering whiteness in a society where whiteness is centric will be challenging. But this is the only pathway to transform our workplaces into the environments that we all deserve.

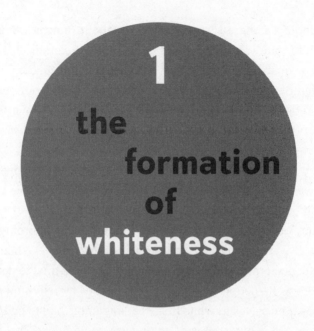

1
the formation of whiteness

Before we dive into the ways that whiteness is centered within the workplace, it's important to first define what whiteness is and how it was created. When I speak about the formation of whiteness, I have to mention that I am speaking primarily from a United States perspective. Although this discussion will be US specific, it is also helpful for those who employ Americans and those with US-based work locations. In the upcoming chapters, when we delve into the ways that whiteness is centered in the workplace, this discussion expands beyond the US and reflects many countries around the world.

I have to admit: I've never been a history person. When I was in high school, history—or social studies, as it was called back then—was my least favorite subject. As I've gotten older and expanded my knowledge about workplace equity, I realize how important history is in any conversation about justice and liberation. In her book *Freedom Is a Constant Struggle*, Angela Davis talks about the importance of developing a shared language to talk about racism. Davis writes, "The call for public conversations on race and racism is also a call to develop a vocabulary that permits us to have insightful conversations. If we attempt to use historically obsolete vocabularies, our consciousness of racism will remain shallow."[1] This chapter is my attempt for us to develop a shared understanding of whiteness and how it was constructed.

In conversations with my friend Joquina Reed, a decolonial educator and workplace consultant, we've talked about white supremacy and how it differs from whiteness. Since white-centering is a tenet of white supremacy culture, it is vital to have a full understanding of whiteness and how it was constructed and developed in the US. When I asked Joquina to elaborate on this, she explained, "It is essential to distinguish that before white people could see themselves as morally superior, they had to see themselves as white first. That apparatus had to be standardized before the manifestation of its premise could occur. That is to say, first came whiteness, and supremacy shortly followed."

The Construction of Whiteness

One phrase that we often hear is that race is a social construct. The racial categories we assign to others are not based on genetics or biology. Theodore W. Allen, an American writer known for his work around white racial identity, argues in his book *The Invention of the White Race* that the white race historically was formed as "an all-class association of European-Americans held together by 'racial' privileges conferred on laboring-class European-Americans relative to African-Americans."[2] As Allen states in his seminal work, "When the first Africans arrived in Virginia in 1619, there were no 'white' people there; nor, according to the colonial records, would there be for another sixty years."

When trying to conceptualize the American idea of whiteness, Nell Irvin Painter, who wrote the book *The History of White People*, states that at the core of our understanding of whiteness is an association between whiteness and freedom. When we think of enslavement, we associate it with racial difference.[3] There wasn't an interest in "white identity" until European-Americans realized, in the seventeenth century, that there were privileges attached to it. In the US, Painter explains, our first notions of whiteness included all male Europeans and their free male children.[4] In 1790, the US Congress stated that only white people could be naturalized as citizens.[5] Painter also brings up the very important and interesting fact that racial oppression is not based or dependent on a person's phenotype (physical characteristics and features), pointing out that the intellectual Gustave de Beaumont considered "Indians and Negroes the very extreme of human wretchedness" but thought of the poor Irish as the worst of both worlds because they lacked the freedom of the American Indian while also lacking security like the American slave.[6]

Painter indicates that as the conception of whiteness began to evolve in the US, the racial hierarchy morphed into Anglo-Saxons being at the top and the Irish right under them. At some point, the Irish would be considered Nordic and were elevated into the upper hierarchy of the US. Slavic immigrants from the Austro-Hungarian Empire, Jews from Russia and Poland, and Italian immigrants had to be judged within the racial hierarchy.[7] Karen Brodkin addresses how the construct of whiteness evolved for Jews in particular in her book *How Jews Became White Folks*, in which she asks: Are Jews a race? Brodkin argues that based on ethnoracial assignment, they are, but notes that they did not assign themselves into a particular category but instead were assigned by American society.[8]

Irish Migration

To understand how white racial identity was formed, we must dive further into the history of Irish immigration to the US. Many of the same people who experienced oppression in Ireland because of their Catholicism were able to absorb the white racial identity in the US, and in doing so became racial oppressors. Noel Ignatiev analyzed how the Irish became white in his book of that name.[9] In the eighteenth century, Irish Catholics were the oppressed group within Ireland and often saw themselves as a "race" rather than a nation. They were prohibited from opening or teaching schools, attending universities, voting or serving in Parliament, and living in certain places. The Irish began immigrating to the United States in large groups in the 1800s, taking up residence in the same neighborhoods and holding many of the same jobs as Black people. Interestingly, a term sometimes used to describe Black people in that time was the "smoked Irish."[10]

According to Ignatiev and others, upon the arrival of the Irish into the United States, intergroup conflict with Black people emerged. Scholars have suggested that the main reason was labor competition. Chattel slavery in the US was "abolished" in 1863, and the Irish and formerly enslaved Africans were now competing for jobs. Ignatiev notes that "white workers organized to defend their caste status, even while striving to improve their condition as workers. They prohibited free Afro-Americans from competing with them for jobs, in effect curtailing their right to choose among masters."[11] The Irish soon learned that in order to enjoy the privileges that they hoped to gain when they arrived in the US, they had to assume the white label and support the subjugation of Black people.

An important point to note, which several researchers, historians, and writers have highlighted, is that two of the primary means through which groups were put into racial categories were the type of labor they engaged in and the neighborhoods they lived in. White as a racial construct cannot exist without "white man's work." White man's work can be conceptualized as work that Blacks were excluded from participating in. Anyone who engaged in white man's work could be thought of as white. Subsequently, no Black person was able to work in the same jobs as the Irish. Whiteness is often thought of in terms of the dichotomy between whiteness and blackness—that is, blackness as the antithesis of whiteness. For Europeans arriving in America, then, the way to assume whiteness and rise within the racial hierarchy was to distance themselves from blackness. Anti-blackness was learned and adopted quickly.[12]

THE EVOLUTION OF WHITENESS

A few months ago, I was scrolling through TikTok, as I've found myself doing more and more as of late, and I came across a video from a creator I follow named @meccavellii. She was discussing antisemitism and what's been going on with Kanye West. She said something about white supremacy that I will quote directly: "The way that white supremacy works, it has to absorb groups to keep advancing and stay in power."[13] I thought a lot about what she said and as I started reading more into the conception of whiteness in the US, her words rang completely true. Whiteness needs and feeds off other groups and communities in order to regenerate and continue to survive and thrive. Part of the reason may be because demographers have predicted that by around the year 2045, the US will be majority non-white.[14] I know this is a thought that worries and frightens many white people. So what are the ways to address this demographic shift? Perhaps the amalgamation of non-white groups to absorb or assume whiteness in order for the race to survive. As we've seen with Irish and Jewish immigrants, whiteness has evolved so much over the years, and we can see changes in who we perceive to be white.

Racialized Groups

At its founding, American society was triracial, including red, black, and white races. In addition to the black/white contrast, there was the red/white contrast. Native Americans, who were considered "red," were stereotyped as being savages who failed to adhere to European customs and norms.[15] In my second book, *The Pink Elephant*, I focused on a few historical events and the important role that they played in othering specific groups. One event I explored was the Trail of Tears, the forced migration of Native American tribes by the US government. Native

Americans were depicted in similar dehumanizing ways as Africans during that time period. Redness became seen as "savage, threatening and unassimilable," Brodkin explains.

As employees from different parts of Europe and Asia began to immigrate to the US for factory work, the racial stratifications classified Asian and European immigrants into similar castes as Black and Native American workers. In the late nineteenth century, as Mexican immigration intensified, working-class Mexicans too experienced racial stigmatization.[16] Around the same time, and another event I explore in *The Pink Elephant*, was the passage of the pivotal 1882 Chinese Exclusion Act, the first race-based immigration legislation in the US.[17] The act was one outcome of the anti-Chinese movement where racial violence was enacted against Chinese people.

In 1965, with the influx of immigrants as a result of the new immigration laws, the Federal Interagency Committee on Education was formed to help develop a racial and ethnic classification system. One result of that committee was the creation of the four racial categories we still use today: American Indian/Alaska Native, Asian/Pacific Islander, Black, and white. A fifth category was later developed for people of "Hispanic" background. The problem with these categories is that they lump unique groups together as one. Based on these racial categories, for example, an individual from the Middle East would be classified as white. Changes are now being made to redefine racial and ethnic categories for greater accuracy. Two examples are the various iterations of the Hispanic/Latino classification and the newly established Middle Eastern North African ethnic (MENA) category.

As Painter notes, American slavery and Black people were central in creating a white identity. Even though our understanding of race continues to expand, the white/black binary prevails. This is why the primary focus of this book is on whiteness and the ways that it is centered. In the upcoming chapters, we'll also explore blackness and the global nature of anti-blackness. Within the US, the conceptions of whiteness differ from other parts of the world. There is still a lack of consensus about what whiteness is and means and who is truly white and non-white.

Race is partially a social construction. As society changes, so do our conceptions of race.

> **NOTE** The US Census Bureau identifies the white race as "A person having origins in any of the original peoples of Europe, the Middle East, or North Africa."[18] When I speak of whiteness in this book, I will use a modified version of the US Census information. Since MENA is becoming its own racial, ethnic, and cultural category, which I think is vastly different from white and European culture, when I refer to white people or the white race in this book, I am referring to *people who originated from Europe.*

2
decentering
whiteness
in hiring
practices

Throughout this book we will explore the ways that whiteness is centered in the different policies, practices, and procedures in the workplace. As a reminder, by "white-centering" I am referring to *actions and behaviors that prioritize, uplift, amplify, and venerate white people and the dominant white culture **above** other cultures and communities.* In this particular chapter, we'll explore how white-centering shows up in our hiring practices. I wanted to start here because our hiring practices play such an integral role in workplace culture; who you invite into the workplace influences the environment. It's much easier to hire the right employees—those who possess inclusive values—than it is to change the behavior of current employees who are deeply invested in centering whiteness.

For the past seven years I've worked in academia, first as an adjunct professor and then moving into a full-time assistant professor role. When I started working as a full-time assistant professor at a private institution in New England, I was teaching in a human resource management master's degree program in a business school. One thing that I found super-interesting was the lack of training that students received in areas like bias. Because the majority of the students that graduated from that program would end up in HR roles within organizations and institutions, it was astonishing to see that the only mention of "bias" was in the diversity, equity, and inclusion (DEI) course that I taught. But bias plays a big role in the talent pipeline, tainting the employment process in various ways. The first part of decentering whiteness in the workplace is decentering whiteness in the hiring process. We first must ask ourselves: What are the ways in which whiteness is centered in the hiring process?

Job Postings

When workplaces are crafting job postings, the default job candidate is white. I had a conversation with someone who worked for the metro system in a major East Coast city in the US. She told me that one of the problems she sees in her company is that candidates from underrepresented racial groups are not being considered for roles because they don't meet all the qualifications on the job posting. To complicate matters more, she said that most of the "requirements" listed aren't even needed to perform the job. It seems as though these requirements currently serve as a barrier to applicants from underrepresented racial groups. She explained that these requirements included specific types of certifications or a degree in particular fields. Many job postings are crafted in ways that unintentionally (or intentionally) prevent certain populations from applying. Some job postings are gendered, and this sends the message to applicants of a particular gender that they are not suited for a role. A 2011 Harvard study found that job advertisements in male-dominated areas contained more male-gendered words compared to female-dominated positions. The researchers also found that gendered wording played an instrumental role in maintaining traditional gender divisions.[1]

Abercrombie & Fitch is a great example of a company that centered whiteness when seeking job candidates in the past. The Netflix documentary *White Hot: The Rise & Fall of Abercrombie & Fitch*, which I highly recommend, confirmed everything I already knew and understood about the company. When I was growing up, Abercrombie was the most popular clothing brand for teens. I never really shopped there because I always got this unconscious feeling that their clothes weren't made for me as a coming-of-age, chubby Black girl. Although I didn't fit the "Abercrombie aesthetic," I still aspired to it. Always being one of the only Black kids in school, I *did* feel like Abercrombie would provide me with the key to ascending in the popularity hierarchy. In the upcoming chapters, I'll dive more into how my deep insecurities led me to center whiteness in a number of ways.

Abercrombie has been routinely called out for discrimination. In 2003, the company was sued for race and sex discrimination.[2] Its primary target customer for many years was "all-American," code for skinny, attractive white Americans. In a 2006 interview Abercrombie's then-CEO, Mike Jeffries, stated, "That's why we hire good-looking people in our stores. Because good-looking people attract other good-looking people, and we want to market to cool, good-looking people. We don't market to anyone other than that."[3] When Jeffries initially made these statements, there wasn't much backlash, but after drawing public ire for them in 2013, Jeffries apologized.[4]

A lot of companies have unspoken rules that are similar to Abercrombie's, where hiring managers are encouraged to hire a specific type of candidate. In job descriptions, they may use racial dog whistles like the previously mentioned "all-American." There's an important point to note here that I emphasize with students when we discuss anti-racist hiring practices. Title VII of the Civil Rights Act of 1964 provides protection against employment discrimination based on race, color, religion, sex, and national origin. Although the legislation is ever-evolving and expanding, *customer preference is never an acceptable reason to discriminate*. If, for example, customers prefer to be helped by white employees and a hiring manager decides to hire *only* white employees in order to appease customers, this is still discrimination. In the next chapter, I'll share an experience I had where a customer refused my service because I am Black.

A blog article from Ongig.com outlines some of the specific ways that these biases show up in job listings.[5] Through coded language, different groups can be discouraged from applying. One example the article cites is the word *Latino*, which is a gendered term and not necessarily inclusive of women, trans, or nonbinary job applicants. Another example is a job ad that encourages "native English speakers." Furthermore, job descriptions that require candidates to be from "top universities" in their particular field (e.g., top university for engineering) may deter students who graduated from historically Black colleges and universities (HBCUs) or lesser-known institutions. Qualities and characteristics that are more common in non-white candidates are often deprioritized. Later in this chapter we will explore how accent discrimination also impacts candidates during the job interview process.

Job postings can create additional barriers for underrepresented racial groups. As mentioned, degree requirements can be one way to push certain populations out, especially if the required degree is in a field or industry where there isn't a lot of racial diversity. Also be aware of specific words that have racial connotations and avoid using them in your job postings. Some examples include *blacklist/whitelist, peanut gallery, grandfathered* and *grandfather clause, cakewalk, lynch mob, uppity,* and *blackball*.[6] Another term that has biased connotations is *third world*.[7] There's also some contention regarding whether a job posting specifying that underrepresented racial groups are preferred is helpful or harmful. On one hand, this is a way to center candidates from underrepresented racial groups. On the other hand, this can lead to tokenism, whereby a workplace hires a candidate only for cosmetic diversity, even if the candidate's background and skill set isn't well aligned with the role.[8]

Another important component of job postings to consider is where the job is actually posted. One of my clients administered a survey to assess where their talent pool was coming from. When advertising open roles in the company, they utilize their company's website, LinkedIn, and Twitter. They found that when job candidates were recruited from the company website or LinkedIn, the talent pool was homogenous and mostly white. Because this particular company is very niche and has a mostly white audience, posting job openings on their website and through LinkedIn was not an effective way for them to attract job candidates from underrepresented racial groups. What we ended up doing was utilizing Twitter and social media in creative ways. We used hashtags to search for candidates from underrepresented communities that worked in the jobs that needed to be filled. We also reached out to "diversity champions" online (folks that were DEI recruiters, DEI practitioners, consultants, etc.) and asked them to share job openings with their networks. On LinkedIn, I'm sometimes asked to do this, so that's where I got the idea. We had to get crafty, but the client was able to get more racial diversity in their talent pool and has slowly been able to hire more employees from underrepresented groups, particularly in the company's more managerial roles.

Decentering Whiteness in Job Postings

Utilize equity consultants to craft or review job postings. Also look into different platforms that strive to remove biased wording from job postings. For smaller companies, an equity consultant or another trained professional can do this by hand. Re-evaluate whether all of the requirements for the role are necessary for the job position. Are you also getting feedback from job incumbents and former job incumbents? What are they saying about the role and the accuracy of the job description? Be flexible with and think about reviewing job descriptions frequently, but especially for roles for which you're having difficulties finding qualified candidates. Also assess exit interview data to see whether there are employees who are complaining about aspects of the role and whether there are racial differences in feedback. When working with companies, I often hear from employees who feel like they're doing things outside of their job role. Are there persistent themes in your exit interview data that reflect this? Review exit interview information frequently to assess whether employees leaving the organization are providing this feedback.

Think about where job openings are being posted. Take one open job role, and make a list of all the places where it is currently being advertised.

Now think outside the box. Are there professional organizations you can use to advertise open roles? A client of mine utilized the directory on a professional networking website for Black lawyers and ended up hiring a candidate they found there. Have you shared a job posting with your online networks? Direct-message those who can amplify a job posting for you or who can help you generate different leads from different racial communities. Share the posting with any professional networks or groups you know of or belong to. It's especially helpful if you're able to find networks and groups for professionals from underserved and underrepresented populations. For lesser-known companies, visibility can be a barrier to attract talent. Smaller companies, nonprofit organizations, and workplaces with fewer resources should be creative and use the tools already available to you (social media, your networks, word of mouth). This can be an effective way to decenter whiteness in your job postings. You'll have to deviate from the norm that you're used to. It will take some effort on your part, but the payoff will be worth it.

Applicant Tracking Systems

Many workplaces utilize an applicant tracking system (ATS) to help them with recruiting candidates. One figure from 2019 indicates that 99 percent of Fortune 500 companies use an ATS.[9] Oracle describes the ATS as a type of software used by employers and recruiters to track job candidates throughout the recruitment and hiring process.[10] Specifically, an ATS helps employers manage applicants, evaluate their qualifications, and identify who is best suited for the job and should move on to the next round. In an ideal scenario, if there are one thousand applicants for a role, the ATS would help narrow this down to a manageable number for employers to interview.

But what's often overlooked is the ways that an ATS can be biased. ATS software was created by imperfect humans and we all have our own inherent biases. This means that bias is baked into the fabric of the ATS, many of which rely on artificial intelligence and machine learning to identify the ideal candidate. An ATS could filter out employees with employment gaps. Not having the "right" degree, or not having a degree at all, could also cause an ATS to eliminate otherwise qualified candidates. It doesn't take into account the financial barriers that many non-white communities face when it comes to getting a college education. It also doesn't take into account the reasons for an employment gap, which could include caretaking, raising a family, having mental health issues, or being incarcerated. More Black and Latin American people are incarcerated than other groups.[11] Incarceration for a petty or nonviolent crime could lead to an employment gap that would automatically disqualify a candidate, since an ATS won't pick up on these important nuances. The software is programmed to unintentionally (or intentionally, depending on whom you ask) prioritize white candidates, making companies more likely to rule out non-white candidates.

Decentering Whiteness in Applicant Tracking Systems

For large companies that get hundreds or thousands of applications, an ATS can make the process much more efficient for hiring managers and recruiters, so it's not realistic to say we should do away with the tool completely. Instead, ensure the process *after* you use the ATS is equitable. Once you have a group of applicants you're interested in interviewing for a role, anonymize their resumes or their CVs so that all the demographic information (name, address, identity-related affiliations, year of graduation) is concealed. An intern can do this for you if there isn't an overwhelming number of applications. There are also systems and programs that you can purchase to anonymize resumes. Instead of or in addition to the ATS, think about utilizing job boards that are targeted to underrepresented candidates. For example, several years ago, I posted my resume on Jopwell, a website that provides a pool of candidates from underrepresented backgrounds.

Hiring Committees

As part of a few hiring committees at a university where I used to work, my role was to evaluate the candidates that had applied through our system. We were hiring for a few different faculty positions within the department. Each time I served on the hiring committee, there were twenty to forty candidates. We were instructed to review their CVs and narrow down the candidates to ten based on their credentials and background. One of the main issues I noticed was that the hiring committee members were given few to no clear criteria regarding what we should be looking for. Each of us went into the interviews prioritizing different qualities in a candidate. I went so far as to create and share a rubric for my evaluations, and while my colleagues seemed to appreciate it, they didn't all use it, so ultimately it worked only to ensure that *my* evaluations weren't biased.

When we went into each interview, we all randomly asked each candidate different questions. Some of our questions had nothing to do with the faculty position. One of my colleagues became engaged in a deep discussion with one of the candidates who shared a similar background. They both were from Canada and spoke French, so that created an immediate connection. They even started speaking a little French to each other. I remember thinking how inappropriate that was, but I didn't say anything because it was my first time taking part in a hiring committee process and I was the only non-white person. Not only were the other committee members all white, but there was a significant age gap between me and the other committee members, who were more seasoned and held senior faculty and administrative positions at the university.

I remember how much work my colleagues and I put in when it came to selecting a candidate for one of the committees I was part of. I was excited because one of the candidates, who was East Asian, was so well rounded and had international experience teaching in Europe. We all agreed that she—let's call her Jane Doe—was ideal for the role. The second-choice candidate was a white woman—we'll call her Mary Sue—who had a good amount of experience but wasn't as well rounded as the East Asian candidate we all favored. The hiring committee was unanimous that Jane Doe was more qualified than Mary

Sue. Unfortunately, the department head decided that Mary Sue was a better fit and we ended up hiring her. The hiring committee was given no explanation regarding why Mary Sue was better. It was a frustrating experience. Looking back, I realize the university was mostly white. I don't know the exact demographics at that time, but according to Google nearly 90 percent of the faculty is white, only about 6 percent is Black, 3 percent is Asian, and the rest of the non-white faculty identifies as multiracial. It's likely that unconscious bias led the department head to "prefer" the white candidate over the more qualified non-white candidate.

Evaluating Job Applicants

Unconscious bias—that is, the unsupported judgments we make about individuals, places, things, or groups—is a pervasive issue that creates barriers to equity in the hiring process. Once a set of job candidates is chosen to move forward, the practices that employers use to evaluate them are often white-centered. As employers evaluate documents like resumes, CVs, and online applications, bias creeps into the process in a number of ways. Name bias is one example. A wealth of studies have found that candidates with Black-sounding names on their resume are less likely to receive callbacks compared to those with white-sounding names. The results of these studies have been replicated with several different racialized groups. People with Arab-sounding names also experience discrimination.[12] And these findings extend beyond the United States—to Sweden, for example.[13]

In addition to name bias, accent bias is a prominent issue. One UK study, published in November 2022, found that people with "foreign accents" were less likely to be nominated for promotions. The researchers found that Afro-Caribbean, Indian, Liverpudlian, and Birmingham accents were rated lower in prestige, and that accent was a primary indicator of a person's socioeconomic status.[14] A 2010 research study similarly found that accents play a vital role in our perceptions about a person.[15] The English language remains the premiere language spoken within the business world and within government. English is more respected in general but particularly American English, British English, and Australian English. An article unpacking this concept of "linguistic racism" noted that "when English is spoken by some Europeans, including for example French-, German-, Italian-accented English, they can be considered really cute, sophisticated, stylish and so forth," but "English spoken by Asians, Africans or Middle Easterners may be viewed as challenging and unpleasant."[16]

Accent bias is an experience my mom has faced continually. Both of my parents immigrated to the United States in the 1980s from the Central and West African country of Cameroon. Upon their arrival, and probably still to this day, they had very thick accents. People often recognize from his accent that my father is West African, but my mom is often mistaken for Caribbean. When my parents lived in Louisiana, sometimes people thought my mom was Creole. Back then, my parents recognized the way that having a non-Native accent created barriers. My dad made a point to discourage my mom from teaching us French, which was the primary language she spoke along with some Native Cameroonian languages. My mom arrived in the US not knowing any English, but my father was adamant about my siblings and me not being labeled as "English as a second language" students. Looking back, although I am eternally grateful to my parents and everything they did to help us assimilate into American culture, I *do* feel like parts of my history, my background, and my culture were destroyed in the process.

In job candidate evaluations, the criterion of culture fit often leads to discrimination. Wanting to hire a candidate that fits the culture of a workplace is not a bad thing, but the methods that are often utilized to assess culture fit tend to be biased and discriminatory. In addition, there's often a lack of clear criteria about what culture fit actually is. Sometimes hiring managers make statements like, "We'll know it when we see it." But everyone has a different understanding and conceptualization of "fit," and leaving it up to each individual employee to determine enables us to lean on our unconscious biases and prioritize white employees or those with *proximity to whiteness*—that is, the physical characteristics and traits that grant someone privileges, power, and access within a white-dominant culture. For example, a biracial person that looks white has a proximity to whiteness that grants them more power than a biracial person that looks Black. A person with a proximity to whiteness, although not white, has some of the privileges, power, and access that comes with whiteness.

Decentering Whiteness in Hiring Committees and Candidate Evaluations

Create a scorecard or rubric before you conduct job interviews so that everyone is on the same page regarding what you should be looking for in a candidate. Utilize structured interview questions and connect each question to a competency that is necessary for the role. To develop a set of competencies, think about all the knowledge, skills, and abilities that are required for a job incumbent to do the job and do it well. Next, develop a set of criteria you will use to evaluate each candidate based on these competencies. Having objective measures by which to evaluate candidates will make the evaluation process much more equitable.

Table 1 is an example of a job rubric for the role of a DEI consultant at a small (two hundred employees or fewer) company. This rubric can also be modified for DEI consultants with no prior experience. It's important to use an even-numbered scale, because evaluators often rate candidates as average. For example, on a 5-point scale with 3 being average, raters may be more inclined to rate candidates as average if they weren't exceptionally good or exceptionally bad. You want to force raters to decide whether candidates were a good fit or not and discourage the use of average scores.

TABLE 1: Sample Interview Rubric, DEI Consultant for Small Organization

FACTORS	CANDIDATES			SAMPLE QUESTION
	#1	#2	#3	
Knowledge of DEI	4	2	3	What knowledge, skills, and understanding have you acquired to help you understand diversity, equity, inclusion, belonging, justice, and accessibility in the workplace?
Relevant skills	4	2	3	What types of organizations and institutions have you worked with in the past and what type of consulting work were you engaged in? (Interview former clients.)
Conflict-resolution skills	3	2	3	How do you help resolve employee conflicts? What are some skills and strategies you lean on when engaging in conflict resolution?
DEI problem-solving	3	2	3	Tell me about a time in the past where you've helped an organization or institution create interventions to resolve the DEI issues they were facing. What was the issue, what was the intervention you helped to develop, and what was the result over time? What impact did that intervention have on the specific DEI issue that the organization or institution was facing?
Self-awareness	2	1	3	On a scale of 1–10, how would you rate your level of self-awareness? What tools do you utilize to learn more about yourself and to develop as a person? How do you address your own shortcomings when it comes to the amount of knowledge and awareness you have about communities outside of your own? How do you address critical/developmental feedback you receive?
Communication	4	2	3	Tell me about a time there was a misunderstanding or disagreement with a client. How did you discuss that issue and how was it resolved?
Total average score	3.33	1.83	3	Candidate 1 is the best candidate for this position according to Rater #1.

1 = Unsatisfactory; 2 = Below average; 3 = Above average; 4 = Exceptional

Job Interviews

White-centering takes place in a number of ways during job interviews. Aside from the fact that white employees are more likely to be advanced through the employment process—as evidenced by the "pipeline problem" that many employers claim is why they're unable to recruit candidates from underrepresented racial groups—white-centering happens during the actual candidate interviews. Wells Fargo recently drew public scrutiny when reports of its hiring policies went public. The company's hiring managers allegedly would conduct "fake interviews" with "diverse candidates" in an effort to appear as if they were prioritizing diversity. These fake interviews were conducted even though the company had already offered the job to other candidates.[17]

Workplaces often engage in performative diversity so that they look like they are hiring "diverse" talent when in actuality, they have no intention of hiring or advancing these candidates. The NFL has also been accused of performative actions through its long-standing Rooney Rule, the policy that requires NFL teams to interview two underrepresented candidates when searching for a head coach. Former Miami Dolphins head coach Brian Flores, who is currently suing the NFL, indicated that it conducted "sham interviews" in order to comply with the Rooney Rule.[18]

During the job interview process, hiring managers from all backgrounds often prioritize white candidates or candidates with proximity to whiteness. This manifests in a variety of ways, including the blatant and subtle racial bias that happens during the interview. These biases are compounded by variables like a non-native accent, body size, age, and attractiveness. For example, the *similar-to-me bias*, also known as the *affinity bias*, means that we are more likely to hire candidates that are like us. For workplaces that are more homogenous and lack racial diversity, candidates that are similar to the hiring managers are more likely to be hired. A lack of racial diversity is likely to affect retention of underrepresented talent, and in turn, the inability to retain underrepresented racial groups will create more difficulties in hiring candidates from these same underrepresented groups. For companies that are mostly white, this is why the "diversity problem" becomes a cyclical issue.

Decentering Whiteness in Job Interviews

Although Title VII of the Civil Rights Act provides protections against discrimination, when racial discrimination takes place during the job interview, it's more subtle and often quite difficult to prove. One of the most impactful ways to remove bias in the job interview is making sure you're implementing a structured interview process and using a set of standard questions to evaluate job candidates. An unstructured interview process is likely to lead to bias. In an unstructured interview, interviewees can ask candidates different questions to gauge their suitability for the role. The problem is that sometimes these questions may elicit bias or cause a candidate to reveal job-irrelevant information about themselves that will hurt them during the interview. Although questions like "Do you have children?" or "Do you plan to have children?" are illegal, if a hiring manager asks a question about an applicant's daily schedule and ability to take on the tasks required for the job, the candidate may mention their childcare responsibilities.

A question like "Where do you live?" isn't illegal per se, but it can elicit racial or national origin bias if a candidate answers the question by giving background on why they reside where they do. Sometimes interviewers rely on the job candidate's lack of understanding and awareness of their rights. Racial discrimination during the employment interview has become more and more difficult to prove. Hiring managers know they can't ask questions about your race or national origin, but even if they do, it would be the candidate's word against theirs and many job candidates don't have the time or energy to pursue a lawsuit with a large corporation or conglomerate. Our unconscious associations often shape the way we perceive candidates, and many of us—even those of us from racially marginalized backgrounds—may possess and internalize negative stereotypes about our own communities. Later in the book, we'll explore internalized oppression and the ways that racially marginalized communities center whiteness.

Try to include as many individuals from different backgrounds into the interview process as possible. Also provide awareness and anti-racism training for employees who are conducting interviews to ensure everyone is on the same page, understands what to be assessing, and recognizes how bias can creep into the interview process.

Referral Hiring

White-centering shows up in organizations' heavy reliance on *referral hiring*, the practice whereby workplaces allow employees to recommend job candidates that they think are qualified for an open role. A few years ago, I was facilitating a workshop for a client. The employee makeup was fairly diverse from a racial and ethnic standpoint, with one of their top executives being a non-white man. During my workshop, I shared that referral hiring should be reconsidered because it often leads to racial bias. Some of my clients have found that their referral programs only reinforced the existing racial disparities within their organization. While I was explaining that particular point during the workshop, the non-white executive interrupted me to say something along the lines of, "I can tell you right now that we use referral hiring to find candidates and we have no intentions of stopping." I had no words when the executive said this; there was an awkward silence in the virtual workshop. Despite my knowledge, skills, and understanding of racial equity in the workplace, it seemed that the executive felt like *he* knew what was best for the company. It might surprise you that a non-white person held such a belief, but later in this book we'll examine why white-centering is just as common in people from racially marginalized backgrounds.

The obvious issue with referral hiring is if the company is homogenous and mostly white, their "diversity issue" won't be solved through referral hiring. Referral programs simply replicate these issues because white people are more likely to know, hang out with, and recommend other white candidates. The traditional referral program structures that I typically see within corporate spaces are often unsuccessful at helping to recruit candidates from underrepresented racial groups.

Even when employees from racially marginalized backgrounds are encouraged to recommend candidates, we have in mind that invisible white audience that Toni Morrison described. Morrison wrote about the white gaze—how we have an invisible white male in mind when we create things. Non-white employees may also be more likely to recommend white employees to open roles in their workplace. A few years ago I was talking with someone about her role as a consultant at one of the big four consulting firms. This person, who identified as South Asian, shared that the firm had a referral program specifically for diverse candidates. As long as she had been working there (a few years at that time), she had never seen the company actually hire someone from an underrepresented racial group. Even though the firm had systems and structures in place like the diverse referral program, they were likely created for performative reasons.

Decentering Whiteness in Referral Hiring

I want to say do away with referral hiring altogether. If that executive I encountered several years ago were reading this, he would disagree! If you decide you want to keep your referral hiring program, center it on targeting employees from underrepresented backgrounds. Avoid tokenization, or hiring for the sake of diversity. Ensure that you're looking for suitable candidates from underrepresented backgrounds whose skills are aligned with open positions. Provide structure for how employees can recommend qualified candidates and frequently review the candidates to assess fit.

Implementing a diverse referral program into the organization but failing to hire any candidates from that pool of referrals can send the message to employees that diversity isn't a priority. If your workplace is struggling to attract candidates from underrepresented racial groups, invite employees into the process to help you. When employees are able to play an instrumental role in developing a workplace practice or process, they have more of a vested interest in ensuring its success. If you decide to keep or create a referral hiring program, be sure you're focused on making it equitable and allow opportunities for employees to be part of the process.

3
decentering whiteness in workplace systems

I worked in banking throughout my undergraduate and graduate years, and our company would always do holiday and birthday celebrations. Our manager would buy a cake for each of our birthdays, and during holidays like Halloween, St. Patrick's Day, and Valentine's Day, we would be asked to dress up or give out items to celebrate. I noticed that one of my colleagues, a Black woman, never participated. At first, I assumed she was just not into holidays. But one day I had a discussion with her and she explained that she was a Jehovah's Witness and her particular religious path didn't celebrate birthdays or holidays of any kind. I remember thinking how wild it was that our company expected and encouraged us to participate in holiday celebrations and traditions without even considering whether these were holidays that employees celebrated. Those who didn't "play along" and engage in corporate celebrations were seen as not being "team players," which would hurt us in the long run, especially when it came time for performance reviews. According to Pew Research Center, over half of all Jehovah's Witnesses in the US (about 64 percent) identify as non-white.[1] According to a 2020 study, 70 percent of Americans identify as Christian, with white evangelical Protestant and white non-evangelical Protestant denominations making up a larger percentage of American Christians.[2] If more white Americans were practicing Jehovah's Witnesses, workplace practices like holiday celebrations would change. Many workplace practices we engage in, often automatically and without much consideration, center whiteness.

Within the workplace, white-centric practices, procedures, and processes that are implemented to carry out workplace tasks and duties—which I will refer to collectively as *workplace systems* for the remainder of this chapter—are one of the main reasons why inequities persist. Any organization or institution that is striving to decenter whiteness must recognize the ways in which workplace systems perpetuate cultures of exclusion, harm, and oppression.

There are several aspects to consider when conceptualizing the workplace system: how employee performance is evaluated, how employees advance and are promoted within a workplace, how employers retain employees, customer service practices, vendor sourcing, and employee work arrangements. In this chapter, we will dive into different elements of the workplace system to explore how whiteness is centered. We'll also uncover some ways that whiteness can be decentered within the workplace system.

White-Centering in Employee Evaluations

In our workplaces, we utilize different tools to evaluate and assess employees. One popular tool used by many organizations is personality assessments. I remember learning about the Five-Factor Model (FFM) in my graduate school programs. Often called the Big Five personality test, the FFM splits our personality up into five traits: extraversion, agreeableness, conscientiousness, neuroticism, and openness to experience.[3] When I took the Big Five personality test for the first time, I felt affirmed; I consider myself a sociable and gregarious person, and when I take the assessment, I always score highly on extraversion. But I never stopped to consider how flawed these personality assessments actually are. The most popular example is probably the Myers-Briggs Type Indicator (MBTI), which some workplaces use during the hiring process (despite its own creators advising against this for ethical reasons) and for team-building and assessing person-job fit. The problem with this and many other personality assessments is that they don't take into consideration disability status or racial, ethnic, and cultural differences and the role that these factors play in our personalities. On top of that, there isn't a lot of solid evidence indicating that these assessments can predict job performance.[4]

No matter the industry or field, evaluating employee performance is an important and vital organizational practice. There are a number of ways to assess employee performance, but many aspects of the process elicit bias. In a traditional corporate structure, employee performance is often measured based on productivity. Productivity can equate to the quantity of a particular product or service being sold to a customer, or being produced by the individual. The higher the quantity sold, the greater employee performance is perceived to be. Time is often a consideration as well. What is the speed at which employees are performing specific tasks, projects, and assignments? Performance can also be measured by behaviors and actions. To mitigate white-centering in employee evaluations, the first step is to think about how employee performance is being assessed within your workplace.

During my time in banking, our performance was measured based on a few different factors. The number of accounts we successfully opened was one example. We would suggest different products and then lead the customer to the banking professionals who could open the accounts. The more accounts we were able to open, the more productive we were as tellers and thus the higher our performance was rated.

Another measure of our performance was the number of errors we made (or the lack thereof). This was based on our accuracy and speed. Being fast with client transactions was important, but accuracy even more so. The fewer mistakes we made, the better our performance was perceived to be. If we worked a shift and the amount in our cash drawer was correct, meaning we had made no errors, this would bode well for our performance evaluations.

Customer satisfaction and service was also an important part of our role. Tellers are the bread and butter of the banking industry. We are the ones who have the most interactions with customers, and we greatly influence customer perceptions about the bank. The bank would periodically reach out to customers after a recent transaction to invite their feedback. We also received feedback through secret shoppers, unidentified bank employees that would periodically visit different branches to assess how the employees interacted with them. One way that whiteness was centered was the lack of racial and ethnic diversity among the secret shoppers who evaluated our performance.

When I was in graduate school, one of the banks I worked at was located in rural Louisiana, about five hours north of New Orleans. When I first started working there, there were customers who had tellers that they "preferred" working with. Some of the customers still used terms like "colored" to refer to Black people. As an employee, my experiences with racism didn't matter as long as the (white) customers were happy. One customer remarked that he did not want me to serve him and preferred to wait for the other teller, who happened to be white. After he left, my colleague explained to me that he was a bit "old-fashioned" and may have had a problem being served by me since I was Black. If I had been the only teller available and he was later asked for feedback on the service he received, his inherent racism and anti-black bias may have caused him to rate me lower than my white peer. This feedback could have impacted my performance reviews and made it seem like I wasn't "performing" as a teller, based solely on one person's shallow and bigoted beliefs. The criteria that we used to evaluate employee performance neglected the role that unconscious biases can play in perceptions and favorability.

I can also draw on my experiences working as a professor for the last seven years. In academia, one of the biggest issues I've seen when it comes to performance evaluations is the inherent bias within student evaluations, which are the main criteria used to assess professor performance thanks to the ease and convenience with which they can be collected. There's a wealth of evidence suggesting that professors from underrepresented racial groups are evaluated less favorably on student evaluations.[5] Despite the research pointing to how biased student evaluations are, universities still place a lot of weight on them. For non-white professors teaching at predominantly white institutions (PWIs), this can make or break your ability to advance and receive promotion or tenure.

Decentering Whiteness in the Performance Evaluation Process

Whiteness is centered in a number of ways in the evaluation of employee performance. The individual or individuals performing the evaluation (managers, directors, students, etc.) come into the evaluation with their own inherent biases. Most leaders across different fields and industries are white, and when they're assessing the performance of people from underrepresented racial groups, their unconscious biases and white-centric lens can impact their evaluations. Simply having more people from racial and ethnically diverse backgrounds performing the evaluations won't completely resolve the issue, but it *can* help. (In the upcoming chapters, we'll dive more into the topic of internalized stereotypes and beliefs.) Make sure that you have more than one person evaluating someone's performance, and if possible, involve people from different racial backgrounds in the process.

Decentering whiteness from the performance evaluation process requires clarity around what competencies are being measured and evaluated for the role that is being performed. Once evaluators have a clear understanding of what each job role entails, they should develop a rubric to evaluate employee knowledge, skills, and abilities. Some companies have a formalized process for evaluating employee performance; this is helpful because it increases objectivity, which in turn can decrease bias. Other workplaces, due to time constraints, a lack of awareness, or apathy, have more subjective processes for assessing performance. Subjectivity opens the door to bias, as each of us reverts to our own white-centric lenses. Are evaluators receiving education around the ways that racial bias impacts the performance review process? There's some evidence that being educated about our bias can have some positive effects in mitigating it.[6] Are those who are engaging in evaluations receiving any ongoing training? In academia, as far as I know, there's little to no education being provided to students about unconscious bias and how it can impact perceptions and evaluations of professors. Throughout this book, I'll outline how education is a vital component to decentering whiteness. Part of the problem is that so many of us don't even realize we are leaning on these white-centered lenses when making decisions.

I've seen organizations utilizing a calibration process to make their performance evaluation system more equitable. With such a process, managers conducting the performance evaluations discuss their employee ratings amongst themselves. The purpose of this process is to ensure consistency and agree on the criteria by which employees are being evaluated. This way, managers can ensure accuracy of performance reviews, mitigate bias, properly reward performance, and create a more transparent evaluation process.[7]

Some important steps to follow to decenter whiteness in the performance evaluation process include:

- Whenever possible, involve people from racially diverse backgrounds.

- Provide education for all evaluators so they understand how unconscious biases can creep into performance evaluations.

- Standardize the evaluation process via rubrics to ensure objectivity.

- Provide ongoing training for evaluators on how to conduct subjective performance evaluations.

- Integrate a performance review calibration process where evaluators are required to discuss their ratings with other raters.

White-Centering in Advancement and Promotion

The promotion and advancement process are also impacted by white-centering. The decision of who gets promoted is often steeped in bias. Whether in a corporate or academic setting, every industry has its own system and process for promoting and advancing employees, often based on factors like tenure and performance. In my consulting work, one trend that I often see is employees not having a clear understanding of how to advance within their organization. I've also witnessed and experienced this in academia. It's no secret that academia is lacking when it comes to racial diversity, and particularly when it comes to Black professors. The public tenure battles of Nikole Hannah-Jones and Cornel West exemplify this issue.

In 2021, a McKinsey report surveyed Black employees in the private sector to get an understanding of the state of Black workers. The report indicates that Black workers face difficulties ascending from entry-level positions into managerial roles, a phenomenon dubbed as the "broken rung."[8] A wealth of research indicates that mentorship and sponsorship play a key role in advancement, particularly for Black employees and other employees from racially marginalized backgrounds. The McKinsey report indicates that Black employees aren't receiving the sponsorships and allyship support they need for advancement. Promotion and advancement strategies should be designed to help the most marginalized. Instead, these strategies are haphazardly implemented in the workplace.

One issue I sometimes encounter with my consulting clients is fears around giving critical or constructive feedback to employees from underrepresented racial groups. Two specific examples come to mind. At one company, there were interpersonal issues between a Black employee and their white manager. The Black employee told me that during their tenure at the company, their manager had not provided them with any developmental feedback. Their manager admitted to me that they could have done a better job providing this employee with feedback. Lacking any developmental feedback, the employee was unable to recognize how to grow and advance in their position and address any areas where they were falling short. Eventually the Black employee resigned. Stereotypes about non-white communities can impact the feedback (or lack thereof) given to employees, which can prevent them from ascending in the workplace.

A few years ago, I was signed up to teach some extra courses in the HR management graduate program where I was teaching full-time. As a clinical (non-tenure-track) assistant professor, I was teaching two or three courses per trimester, or about seven courses each academic year. One day the program director emailed me saying we needed to have a serious conversation. When we got on the phone, he told me that a few students had said they weren't enjoying my classes, and that they "weren't learning" from my course. I was shocked to hear this feedback. The program director asked some follow-up questions to get a deeper understanding of my course structure. I replied that I assigned students articles to read that were relevant to the topics we were discussing each week. During class, we would discuss the readings and then I would pose a series of questions to students to further explore the applications of the reading. When I explained this, the program director seemed perplexed. He told me that this approach was called the Socratic method and that it was the *exact same* method he was using in his courses. I remember him saying something along the lines of, "I wonder why they have a problem with *your* course if they don't have any issues with mine." I knew exactly why.

After this conversation, I invited the program director to review my course videos. As a technophile, when I found out that the classroom where I was teaching was able to record my lectures and save them in a portal for students, I was excited. I created several trimesters' worth of recorded lectures. I asked the program director if he could review them and provide me with any instructional or developmental feedback that he felt would improve my teaching, and he agreed. He never got back to me, which I assumed meant he had no developmental feedback for me (or that he didn't review the videos).

My mind didn't immediately jump to racism in that situation. It didn't until I shared what happened with my partner, who asked me if I thought bias was influencing student perceptions of my course. The only difference between me and the program director was that I was a Black woman in her early thirties and my boss was a white man in his late fifties. I was even using the same syllabus as he was, just modifying it slightly. When he stated that he taught his courses in the *exact same way* as I did, that confirmed to me that there was something else at play. As ironic as it sounds, even as a workplace equity consultant who owns her own DEI consultancy, I didn't initially assume that racism could have been the culprit.

A few weeks later, I received a message from the department chair. (For those of you not familiar with the world of academia, the program director is like my immediate manager, and the department chair is his manager.) She told me that the same students who'd complained to the program director about my teaching had also come to her, using the same narrative about how they were "not learning" from my courses. When the department chair asked whether they had spoken to me directly about their concerns, they told her that they were "too scared" to talk to me. Without any further discussion, the department chair decided to remove the course from my schedule, with only a few days' notice before the new trimester was beginning. There was no conversation with me about the veracity of these students' claims and no acknowledgment of the pervasiveness of racial bias within academia. The immediate assumption was to center and prioritize the feelings of these white students. Although I wasn't given their names, it was easy to figure out which students had complained via process of elimination. One student was angry with me for not allowing them to submit late assignments after the trimester was over. They had complained to the program director about me, and I'd been given feedback about that student just the trimester prior. It was clear that the student had rallied the other students from the program to express their "concerns" because of a personal vendetta they had against me for not letting them turn in their assignments late.

In that experience, whiteness was centered in very distinct ways. The feelings of the white students were centered and prioritized over mine as the professor, despite any institutional "power" I held as a professor. The university didn't have any conversations with me as a professor, and the program manager and department chair (who were both white) also believed the students' claims without stopping at any moment to question whether the students could have been biased. Direct actions were taken to "discipline" me for my inadequate performance. A few months later, the department chair brought up the situation during my performance evaluation, and she also left developmental feedback about the incident on my performance review.

There are often perceptions that Black women, for example, are aggressive and will react negatively to feedback. The angry Black woman stereotype is something I've written about in detail.[9] The racial microaggressions I had experienced for years while at that particular institution prompted me to leave. I am not alone in what I experienced. It didn't cross leadership's mind that the claims from the students could have been based on unconscious racial biases they held. These situations happen so often to non-white employees and impact their ability to advance and get promoted within organizations and institutions.

Decentering Whiteness in Advancement and Promotion

When thinking about strategies for promoting and advancing employees, we must acknowledge how often white employees are centered and prioritized. This is evident when I consult with organizations and ask them about retention and turnover numbers. I'm often given data that isn't disaggregated; all employees, regardless of the racial and ethnic background, are lumped together. Why not parse out the data and look at demographic trends? Are there similar rates of turnover for Black employees compared to their counterparts? What about Black women employees? Or Indigenous employees? Retention methods must be specific and targeted to underrepresented communities. When developing strategies to retain employees or even attract customers, companies always center white people. The white employee or customer is always the archetype. Decentering whiteness in the advancement and promotion process will require:

- Considering the ways that unconscious bias impacts perceptions of a non-white employees.

  Asian employees, for example, experience challenges when it comes to advancement. They face an invisible barrier, which has been dubbed the "bamboo ceiling," when it comes to advancement: because of stereotyping and biases, they are often misjudged as not possessing the traits generally associated with leaders.

- Using multiple feedback sources to evaluate the employee. Is there an understanding of the ways that these feedback systems can be biased? (I recognize that *all* feedback systems are biased to an extent, but the goal is to make them as unbiased as possible.)

- Examining what inequities exist due to historic marginalization, and how that manifests itself in your workplace.

  The "Black tax," for example, is the phenomenon in the Black community where Black employees are expected to use their earnings to help family members financially.[10] Because of factors like the Black tax, although a Black employee and a white employee may be getting paid the same amount, the way that their money must be allocated can differ. If, for example, you're utilizing cash bonuses as a way to reward employee performance, be aware of how race and ethnicity impact this particular reward model. Don't assume that your employee reward system will engage *all* employees; take racial differences into consideration. Assuming that there's a blanket strategy to increase employee engagement and motivation neglects how historical marginalization has affected different communities. Examine the hierarchies within your workplace and determine who are the most vulnerable and marginalized populations of workers. What systems could you develop to address their specific needs when it comes to advancement and support? Asking this question will help you determine the ways in which white-centric norms are baked into your organization.

Some additional questions to ask when decentering whiteness in your workplace's promotion and advancement system include:

- Who is evaluating employee performance and why?

- How many employees are evaluating performance? Is there racial and ethnic diversity among them? (Think beyond "diversity of thought.")

- Is the source of feedback able to provide an objective perspective? (Or at least as objective as possible.) Training can help with this.

- Outside of the performance evaluations and reviews, how is employee feedback given?

- Are employees given the opportunity to also evaluate their leaders and those who manage them?

White-Centering in Customer Service Practices

Customer-facing businesses also engage in white-centric practices when it comes to addressing customer needs. Most companies have white customers in mind and prioritize their needs over the needs of their non-white customers. I saw this with one of my clients, a very niche company that caters to a specific and very white demographic. The majority of its customer base happens to be white women. I was sitting in a meeting with that client one day and an employee (who happens to be non-white) remarked how the company is interested only in creating products that cater to its white demographic. When I probed leadership about this, they indicated that though this was somewhat true on the surface, it wasn't that simplistic. The leaders explained that they have to create products that meet the needs of their *current* customers because they don't want to lose them. Rather than focusing on attracting new customers from more racially and ethnically diverse backgrounds, they wanted to focus on the customers they already had.

As a for-profit business, you have to engage in business practices that allow you to be sustainable. My client felt that without catering to its current consumers, the company wouldn't be sustainable. I explained that expansion was impossible if the company didn't *also* consider how to design a product that had different communities and populations in mind. Those two variables—catering to current customers while also striving to attract new ones—don't have to be at war with each other. Within a lot of organizations and institutions, the default is the white customer. Within the next twenty to thirty years or so, the United States will be majority non-white. No company will be sustainable if it fails to consider the needs of non-white communities.

Even within companies that were created with a Black audience in mind, the white audience, or what Toni Morrison labeled "the white gaze," is ever-present. SheaMoisture is a haircare brand that was created for Afro-textured, kinkier hair. Started by Richelieu Dennis and his mom, the brand skyrocketed to popularity in the 2010s because there were few products on the market at the time that catered specifically to Afro-textured hair. In 2017, the company drew public ire after airing a commercial that did not feature any Black women.[11] The women in the commercial shared stories of experiencing prejudice because of their hair. One woman, who appeared to be white, even shared a story about being treated differently because she was a redhead. The company, which had been marketed primarily to Black women, didn't include any unambiguously Black women in its commercial. This led many to believe that SheaMoisture had neglected its core audience, who had been primarily responsible for the company's success.

The same issue occurred with the Black haircare brand Mielle Organics. In early 2023, the brand received both praise and criticism for its partnership with Procter & Gamble Beauty. Many of its Black consumers worried that the formula would change and the products would no longer cater to Black hair. Others questioned why Black-owned businesses always have to partner with or get acquired by white-owned companies to be seen as successful.[12] Many non-white business owners may hide or shield the fact that they are not white-owned and even use marketing and advertising materials that showcase white people as a means of catering to and centering white audiences. White is *always* the default.

Decentering Whiteness in Customer Service Practices

Any workplace that wants to grow and thrive in the future must be thinking beyond the default white consumer. The customer bases you'd like to attract have to be catered to specifically. The world is in a space where people desire to see more representation in any form and fashion. The success of movies like *Crazy Rich Asians* and *Black Panther* provides evidence of how hungry consumers are for diversity. Decentering whiteness in your customer service practices requires you to think deeply about these questions:

- Who is our current customer base?
- What are the racial and ethnic demographics of our consumers?
- What consumers from underrepresented populations are we missing? What specific strategies can we implement to cater to this specific demographic?
- Who can help us with these targeted strategies?
- Are there customer service practices we've been engaging in that prevent us from attracting non-white consumers? Evaluate where you advertise and market your product or service. Are you, for example, marketing and advertising on websites with mostly white audiences?

Consider conducting research with focus groups to gauge perceptions of your product or service from different audiences and solicit feedback about strategies you could be utilizing to improve your product or service. Typically, a trained professional will lead the focus group in a discussion based on a series of questions designed to gather information. Utilize focus groups as a way to decenter whiteness in your customer service practices. Also assess the teams you already have in place to develop marketing and public relations campaigns. An unsurprising pattern I've noticed after companies find themselves in hot water for a racist marketing campaign is that the folks who were instrumental in developing it are mostly white.

Several years ago, a well-known fashion brand invited me to moderate a panel for its global conference in Europe. It was my first time being flown out internationally by a major corporation, and I was excited to participate and ask the corporate executives some hard-hitting questions about their DEI methods. One question I was eager to ask was about a gaffe that the company had recently committed when it placed racist imagery on a product. The company experienced severe public backlash and consumer boycotts. I wanted to get a better understanding of how that situation could have happened in the first place. What I discovered was that the team that developed the products was Europe-based and all white. The racial and cultural nuances that Americans, for example, are aware of don't necessarily translate when you go to other countries. There was a complete lack of awareness regarding the racist origins of certain symbols and imagery. A large part of the problem was that, prior to that incident, the company didn't have an adequate system of checks and balances in place to assess whether products that were being created were inclusive, fair, and just. Because white consumers are the default, these sorts of oversights happen often. We've seen this scenario replicated in a number of other fashion houses. It's imperative to ensure that the teams creating and approving products are racially and ethnically diverse.

4

decentering whiteness in workplace policies

Workplace policies are the guidelines that dictate appropriate workplace conduct and best practices.[1] Organizations and institutions typically have a handbook that outlines specific conduct that is expected of employees. Workplace policies must be ever-expanding to keep up with the rapidly changing environment. Ten years ago, few organizations had explicit policies related to social media, for example. In this era, when someone says or does something inflammatory, people flock to their social media pages to see who they are and where they work to urge their employer to fire them for their transgression. A company today would be irresponsible if it didn't have any language regarding social media conduct and expectations around usage. It's important to have clearly laid-out policies that employees are expected to adhere to, particularly policies that are racially equitable. As you'll learn in this chapter, many of our workplace policies center whiteness in different ways.

White-Centering in Customer Service Policies

Most companies don't explicitly say, "We value profits over our non-white employees," but their actions clearly indicate that they do. One of my past clients was a well-known global company that asked me to lead a series of workshops for some of its teams. While in the workshops, employees revealed one of their gripes with the organization. They explained to me that there were detailed and thorough policies for how employees were expected to resolve and de-escalate customer complaints. The employees were well versed on how to resolve customer conflicts and issues. The problem was that there *wasn't* this same clarity—or any specific policies at all—around resolving issues when customers treated the employees poorly. This discrepancy was further complicated by racial dynamics on the team that centered whiteness.

In one of these workshops, a Black employee shared with me that she had been harassed by a white customer, and the company did little to resolve the issue, taking no disciplinary action against the customer because he was a big spender at the company. The company had shown that it prioritized the customer over the safety of its Black employee. The employee also felt like racial and power dynamics were at play, with her being a young Black woman and the customer being an older white man contributing to the company's lack of response. Not only that, but a similar incident had occurred when a white female employee was harassed by a customer, and the company's response had been quite different: it took swift actions against the customer who had harassed the white employee. This same protection wasn't extended to the Black employee. Yes, there should be policies that protect the customers from experiencing harm *but also* clear and transparent policies that protect employees, especially non-white employees, and hold perpetrators of racial harm accountable.

It's time we do away with the "customer is always right" mantra. It can actually prove harmful. As someone who spent a lot of my youth working in retail, I experienced mistreatment at the hands of customers who were abusing company policies because they knew that their status, clout, wealth, and whiteness allowed them to do so. Retail was a nightmare. I always tip my hat to people that work in the retail and service industries. I've also worked in the latter, and the prevailing ideology in both industries is that the customer's wants, needs, and desires take precedence over employees. Power dynamics further subjugate racially marginalized employees. The "customer is always right" mantra unfairly impacts non-white employees. The customer is *not* always right, especially when they're causing racial harm to employees, but for many organizations, if the customer is adding to the bottom line, the harm they're causing doesn't matter. In the time I spent as both a waitress and a retail employee, I was working with mainly non-white people but serving mostly white people. My feelings didn't matter as long as the customer was happy. When I would report the mistreatment I experienced to leadership, my feelings, thoughts, and concerns were not taken seriously.

A friend of mine experienced this within her university. For context, she is a Black millennial woman in her thirties who worked as a professor in a large university in New York City. She had a student who wanted to receive an accommodation to retake a test. She explained to the student she was flexible and available for several days leading up to their winter break, but not after a specific date because she had an international flight scheduled and she had to submit grades before she left. The student, apparently angry that they couldn't take the test during the times *they* preferred, found out my friend's address and her family's information and doxed her in a WhatsApp group chat with other students from the university. Another student alerted my friend to the situation. My friend told me this story as it was happening in real time, and I was both worried and pissed off for her. I asked her for information about the student to try googling them, but we found nothing about the student online. My friend's course was hybrid, so in-person attendance wasn't required. She knew very little about remote students because some of them didn't turn their camera on during class sessions. She complained about the student to university administration as she was worried for her safety, especially since she was teaching on campus and this student clearly had a vendetta against her. To make matters worse, she had no idea what this student looked like and the university wasn't able to provide much information. The administration didn't seem to care about my friend's concerns, even though they had the student's name and information.

Academia has an alarming number of policies that are white-centric. This same friend had another horrific experience that I ended up sharing on social media to see if anyone could help her. She received an email from an anonymous sender (perhaps the student that had doxed her in the WhatsApp group) calling her the n-word among other racial epithets and expletives. When she reported the email to her university, she was told that there wasn't much they could do because the sender had sent the email through a server that allowed them to shield their identity. Even after my friend told administrators she didn't feel safe on campus, they *still* forced her to teach in-person, where she had over one hundred students enrolled in her courses. The university was more concerned about having the enrollment numbers that it needed than the safety of the professor. There were a number of policies in place for when students experienced harm, but very few policies for employees who experienced racial harm. In my experiences consulting with and working within academia, when white professors are in positions and situations where they feel unsafe, *their* safety and protection is often prioritized. My friend and I both agreed that had she been a white woman, there likely would have been more urgency and concern for her situation. There were no consequences in both of those incidents. Many workplace policies don't provide a shield for individuals that experience racial harm.

I understand that for-profit businesses need consumers in order to be viable. But pedestalizing and prioritizing the needs of white customers (and white students) over the feelings and protection of non-white employees will prevent these companies from being sustainable. One consistent theme I see when conducting qualitative analyses to assess workplace culture is employees noting that there are protections and policies in place to make sure (white) customers are safe and protected, but none in place for employees, especially those from racially marginalized backgrounds—just as we saw earlier with the Black female employee who was harassed by a white male customer.

When I was working as a bank teller, I was robbed. I was working at a location in a mostly white area and was the only non-white person working there. Bank robberies are actually pretty rare, but banks still train each employee on what to do in the event it happens. The day I was robbed, a man came into the bank and slipped me a note telling me he had a gun and to empty out my cash drawer. During on-the-job training, tellers are instructed to give a cash dye pack, a pack of money that has ink dye hidden in the middle and is triggered to explode once the robber walks a certain distance away. The money is then colored by the ink, alerting people to the fact that it was stolen. When the robber came up to me, I did exactly as the note instructed, giving him as much cash as I could from my cash drawer, but in my panic I forgot to give him the cash dye pack. I did remember to push the alarm, which automatically alerts the corporate office that there's an issue so they can contact the local police. I remember when I told my colleagues I had just been robbed. I was so shaken up, probably in shock. The first thing the assistant branch manager asked me wasn't whether I was okay, but whether I gave the robber the cash dye pack.

Apparently, my safety wasn't as important as making sure they caught the robber, who didn't steal a substantial amount of money. When the police arrived, they spent the next few hours asking me questions about the identity of the robber and what I could remember. One police officer even insinuated that I could have known the robber since he was Black and I was Black. I will never forget that. I wondered to myself: If I were white and the robber were white, would these same insinuations be hurled at me? I highly doubt it. And while the robbery had little to do with race, how I was treated afterward did not make me feel protected or safe. It felt like my managers cared more about why I didn't adhere to the policy of putting the cash dye pack in the robber's bag than my mental state and well-being. I also thought about what safety and protection I had as the only Black person working in that bank. If I had given the robber the cash dye pack and he escaped, would he come back for me? All of these thoughts were racing in my head. At the time, I was a single woman living alone in an apartment in a capital city, and I was worried about all the possibilities. If the robber came back or found out who I was, who would protect *me*?

Decentering Whiteness in Customer Service Policies

I often find that there simply aren't policies in place that offer protections for non-white employees or even non-white customers. In 2018, Starbucks was in the headlines for the arrest of two Black men. A white manager had called the police on two Black men who were in a Philadelphia Starbucks for a meeting. The manager told these men that they couldn't be in the location if they didn't order anything and then called the police on them, resulting in their arrest.[2] From an outsider's perspective, there may have been a desire to prioritize the needs of white customers and the feelings of the white manager over the needs, desires, and dignity of those two Black men. There is a plethora of viral stories of Black customers being followed, mistreated, or ignored while shopping. The Black customer is rarely at the forefront of one's mind.

Think about the different ways that racial harm can manifest in your workplace. An important question to consider is: What protections do you have in place that provide safeguards for customers, especially those from racially marginalized backgrounds? Make sure there are clear-cut policies that provide protection for consumers, customers, employees, and leadership. Ask employees for feedback about this as well. Looping employees into this process can make them feel more involved and included in employment decisions; everything doesn't have to come from the top and trickle down. Rather, think about ways to include employees more and frequently assess their perceptions to ensure that your customer service policies are including and prioritizing people from racially marginalized backgrounds. Also consider feedback you've received from customers about your policies. Do you collect demographic data about customers, and have you ever tried to segment the data to figure out whether there are racial differences in your customer experience? Start to assess the customer experience and consistently request feedback from both your customers and employees about ways to improve the experience and whether more inclusive policies could be implemented.

White-Centering in Specific Workplace Policies

Many seemingly neutral workplace policies are white-centric. Some specific workplace policies to reassess include appearance, employee leave, and health insurance policies.

Appearance Policies

Attorney Leah Goodridge wrote a compelling piece for the *UCLA Law Review* about how professionalism is a tool used to "subjugate people of color in the legal field" and a metric to police and regulate characteristics of non-white people.[3] Your workplace may unknowingly have policies that are exclusionary against non-white employees. Abercrombie & Fitch found itself in this situation when the company refused to hire a woman who was wearing a hijab, the head scarf worn by Muslim women. The woman that had applied for the role, Samantha Elauf, ended up suing Abercrombie for religious discrimination in hiring, which is a violation of Title VII of the Civil Rights Act of 1964. Abercrombie claimed that Elauf's black head scarf went against its dress code. The case went to the US Supreme Court, which ruled in Elauf's favor.[4]

Company policies on grooming, dress code, and appearance often disadvantage (whether unintentionally or intentionally) non-white employees. For many workplaces, hair, and more specifically Black hair, is a topic of contention. Black hair is often seen as unruly and unprofessional. That was the case for Brittany Noble Jones, a local newscaster in Jackson, Mississippi. When her signature bob hairstyle started damaging her hair, Noble Jones decided to switch to her natural hair. She was told by management that her natural hair looked "unprofessional" and that she needed to "tame her fro," and eventually she started wearing wigs to comply with workplace policies. Noble Jones alleges that she was ultimately terminated because of her hairstyle choices and filed a case with the Equal Employment Opportunity Commission.[5]

There is a history of seemingly neutral policies having a disparate impact on non-white employees. A pivotal example occurred in the early 1990s, when a Domino's Pizza policy was found to be discriminatory against Black men.[6] The policy restricted Domino's delivery drivers from having beards. On the surface, this was a seemingly neutral grooming and appearance policy, but the company had white employees in mind when they created it. Black men are more prone to a skin condition where shaving causes inflammation and razor bumps.[7] Domino's argued that the policy was in place because customers preferred unbearded delivery drivers, but customer preference isn't an acceptable rationale. The policy was later found to be discriminatory and Domino's eventually changed it.

Bereavement Leave Policies

A few years ago, I was scrolling through LinkedIn and saw a post about a company's bereavement policy, which wasn't inclusive of different cultures. In the post, Namitha Jacob shared an experience where her eldest uncle had passed away and she requested time off to attend his funeral. Her supervisor told her the company's bereavement leave policy included only immediate family members and step-siblings. However, as Jacob explained in an interview I conducted with her after I saw her post, "in Indian American culture . . . divorce is really rare." She told me, "I saw many facets of family represented [in my company's policies], but I didn't see uncles and aunts represented. And to me in my family . . . my uncles and aunts are absolutely my immediate family." Her company had created a seemingly neutral policy that actually centered the white American family structure to the detriment of other cultures.[8]

In a recent group chat with my friends, we started talking about how half-siblings are seen differently within white families and non-white families. This conversation was particularly fascinating for me because of the clear dichotomy that I witnessed growing up when it came to some of my white friends who had half-siblings; I would notice there was often a clear distinction or delineation when a family member was a half-sibling. When you share one parent with someone, the family dynamics can be different depending on your culture, race, and ethnicity. I never really thought about these dynamics until having this group chat with my friends, and it made me think about the workplace and how often company policies don't consider anything but a "traditional" (read: white) family structure.

When I traveled to Japan several years ago, I learned that it's common for grandparents to live in the home with their children and grandchildren. Multiple generations are living under one roof. In American culture, it's more common for the elderly to be sent to nursing homes. When reflecting on this, I realized that many friends of mine, both in the Black and the Latine community, were raised by their grandparents, and their grandparents played a pivotal role in their lives compared to those of white peers that I've gone to school with. A few years ago, the grandmother of one of my best friends passed away from Covid-19. My friend took time off for bereavement, but when she asked her employer for additional time off to grieve, her employer denied it. My friend had been raised by her grandmother. Despite this, her employer refused her request and demanded (during the height of the Covid-19 pandemic, by the way) that she come back into the office. My friend ended up quitting a few months later.

Health Insurance Policies

White-centering is also very apparent in our healthcare policies in the US. Although this isn't something that workplaces have direct control over and is often determined by health insurance companies, it deserves mention. Many health insurance policies are centered on the white traditional family unit or what's deemed the nuclear family, and don't consider family structures and dynamics that are more common among people of the global majority. On LinkedIn, someone wrote a comment that has stuck with me. The person explained that they are the sole care-taker for their ailing grandparent, but their insurance plan prohibited them from adding their grandparent as a dependent. Health insurance plans typically allow you only to add a current spouse and children as dependents. In the US when we consider dependents, we don't account for the people who are caring for aging parents or grandparents. As mentioned, grandparents are an important part of the household in many different cultures, but US health insurance policies remain firmly centered on the white family.

Decentering Whiteness in Your Workplace Policies

We must rethink what we consider to be "professional." It's important to peel back the layers. What does professionalism actually look like? How do we conceptualize it? What behaviors and actions must be embodied, and why is this important for the role? Having very clear operational definitions for our expectations is vital. I remember only a little from the many research methods courses I took during my PhD program, but one point that was always emphasized was the importance of *operational definitions*, "a description of something in terms of the operations (procedures, actions, or processes) by which it could be observed and measured."[9] In other words, when you decide on the variables you want to measure for a study, you must figure out how they are being defined. Having a clear operational definition will help you ensure that you're actually measuring what you intended to measure.

Clarity and transparency around policies is vital. When I work with organizations and institutions, one pattern I see is policies in place without any explanation or rationale behind them. Employees sometimes tell me that certain policies have been in place for eons, but they don't understand why. Reconsider your legacy policies—those policies that have been around for years or even decades—and ask yourself these questions:

- Why is this specific policy in place?

- How are we operationally defining the actions and behaviors that are related to different policies?

- Is this policy inclusive of employees from different racialized populations?

Do you consider different family dynamics and structures when creating bereavement and family-friendly workplace policies? How long is your bereavement leave? Does it take into consideration flight times? To fly to Cameroon, for example, it can take up to twenty-four hours with layovers and stops. If your bereavement leave policy only grants employees up to one week off, it's not inclusive of people whose families are outside of your country and who may need several days just to travel to a location.

Consider inviting an equity consultant or HR business partner to review your workplace policies to assess for equity. In addition to periodic policy reviews, invite employees to provide feedback about workplace policies so you can determine which are ineffective and inequitable. By allowing employees to be part of the policy ideation process, you're letting them know they're important and valuable contributors to the organization. Being instrumental in the creation or evolution of workplace policies can make employees feel more invested in the organization. Contemplate how this could be structured in your workplace.

White-Centering in Employee Work Arrangements

Post-pandemic, there has been an urge and push from corporate leaders to get employees back into the office. Since the fall of 2020, we've been hearing rumblings of organizations that will be mandating back-to-office work arrangements. In his 2022 State of the Union address, President Biden stated that it was time for employees to go back to the office and that things were finally "safe."[10] *New York Times* best-selling author Malcolm Gladwell received backlash and scrutiny in the summer of 2022 after arguing that remote work was harming society.[11] Many leaders who are encouraging a return to the office are neglecting the research evidence indicating that a majority of employees prefer remote and hybrid work environments over fully in-office work arrangements.

Work arrangement policies must be decentered from whiteness. In 2021, a Future Forum study found that 97 percent of Black workers surveyed preferred remote or hybrid work versus fully in-person work arrangements.[12] Many Black employees and employees from other racially marginalized groups experience fewer microaggressions when working in remote settings. For many racially marginalized employees, this can motivate their desire for remote work arrangements. Leadership ignores this data and has decided that the needs and desires of management supersede the needs and desires of employees. As we've seen, leaders often care only about the bottom line and prioritize profits over people. Work arrangement policies are often white-centric and prioritize white employees. Have you thought about how a return to the office will affect employees from underrepresented racial groups? Sometimes what's good for the company's pockets (or seemingly good) is at odds with the needs and desires of the most marginalized employees.

Decentering Whiteness in Employee Work Arrangements

One of the main ways to decenter whiteness in employee work arrangement policies probably sounds overly simplistic. Not enough workplaces are actually taking into consideration the needs and desires of employees. Many workplaces are concerned about the unused office space and want to be able to surveille employees because of a perceived lack of trust. Try to find a happy medium where employees are able to thrive but employer needs are also addressed. Think honestly about this question: Why is it necessary to come back to the office? Develop a short survey and see what employees' preferred work arrangement is, then ask for their help to brainstorm how to make it possible. Workplace policies shouldn't be created only by those in power. Anyone who will be affected by workplace policies should play a role in their creation or modification. Think about ways to loop employees into the process.

If your company has an affinity group or an employee resource group, think about ways to allow members to be part of the employee policy creation and modification. Every workplace policy should be developed with the most harmed and vulnerable employee in mind; operating from this mindset is how you will decenter whiteness from your workplace policies.

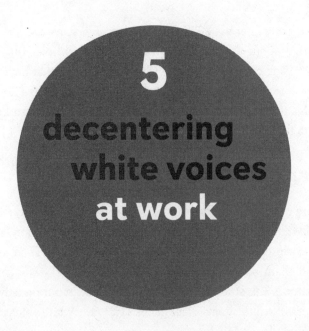

5

decentering
white voices
at work

What is meant by "white voices"? And what does it mean to decenter them in the workplace? When I say "white voices," I'm referring to any viewpoints that reflect and uphold white-dominant cultural values, norms, and mores. The term doesn't refer only to white people in the workplace; it also reflects *the ways that non-white people amplify, deify, and venerate the voices of white people and white-dominant culture*. White people are not needed for white voices to be amplified and centered.

Chris Rock recently did a Netflix comedy special that has been receiving some backlash. The public hadn't heard Rock talk extensively about being slapped by Will Smith at the 2022 Academy Awards until the Netflix comedy special. As I scrolled through social media, I saw transcripts of Rock calling Smith's wife, Jada Pinkett Smith, the b-word. One particular statement Rock made during the comedy special piqued my interest. He said, "You know what my parents taught me? Don't fight in front of white people."[1] That statement was similar to the commentary

I heard directly after the 2022 Oscars when everyone was sharing their perspective about the incident. I saw some Black folks on my social media timeline complaining about how Smith shouldn't have behaved that way in front of "mixed company." Whether we realize it or not, we are always mindful and cognizant of this invisible white audience and allow it to dictate our lives in a number of ways.

How White Voices Are Centered

How were people like Bernie Madoff, Elizabeth Holmes, Billy McFarland (the con artist who cofounded the Fyre Festival), and Shimon Hayut (the "Tinder Swindler") able to scam so many people? Their whiteness protected them and allowed them to be seen as knowledgeable and trustworthy. A 2011 study found racial disparities in our perceived trustworthiness of white versus Black faces.[2] How are white voices centered in your workplace? Meetings are a common place where white voices are centered. Non-white employees sometimes report feelings of invisibility or being ignored for their contributions. Asian employees, and more specifically East Asian employees, often recount experiences of feeling invisible in the workplace.[3] There are also a number of studies where Black women employees report feelings of invisibility.[4] When non-white employees *do* contribute thoughts during meetings, their contributions are more likely to be overlooked and ignored.

Once I was working with a corporate client that had just implemented an employee resource group (ERG). ERGs are typically groups of people within a workplace who have some sort of shared identity— for example, Muslim employees, Black employees, LGBTQIA+ employees, or veteran employees. This particular client wanted the ERG to be for non-white employees. At some point, I suggested that the company keep the group closed and prohibit white employees from joining, since its purpose was to be a safe space for underrepresented racial groups in the workplace. The leaders thanked me for this suggestion but ultimately felt that they knew what was best for their employees and decided to open up the ERG to all employees who wanted to join.

Fast forward to a few years later, and the client shared with me that the ERG was being disbanded because it had devolved from its original purpose and many of the members felt like they weren't making an impact. When looking back at that situation, I think a large part of the issue was that white employees were able to join the ERG, and despite their best intentions and efforts, it changed the dynamic of the group. ERG members from underrepresented racial groups had come to expect that the ERG would be instrumental in changing company policies and practices. The irony of the situation is that when I, their Black woman DEI consultant, advised them that the group should be kept closed, the leaders (who all happened to be white) decided against my suggestion and felt that they knew what was "best" for the organization.

The ways that white voices are centered in the workplace are often so inconspicuous, which makes the issue much harder to address. In the moment, I didn't think much of the situation with my client's ERG. It wasn't the first time that I've given clients suggestions that they ignore, overlook, or decide against. That's the push and pull of consulting work; clients always have the right to disagree or decide against my advice. But when I engage in DEI work, I root my consulting not only in my lived experience as a Black woman, but also in the research, knowledge, and understandings that I've acquired from working with different companies and institutions and learning about the lived experiences of marginalized and oppressed groups. To bring me in as a subject-matter expert and then ignore my advice is just one example of the ways that white voices are centered in the workplace.

Decentering White Voices during Meetings

White voices being centered and prioritized in the workplace is a pervasive issue that every organization and institution deals with, and it's imperative to recognize opportunities to counteract it. It shows up in several ways, as we've discussed, but particularly during team meetings. Non-white employees often feel like they have to shrink themselves because their voices are not heard—there are several pervasive stereotypes that also accompany being outspoken as a non-white person.

One strategy you can use to address the centering of white voices during meetings is the round robin technique. I'm not sure who came up with this technique, but I rarely see it being used during employee meetings. Each person is given a specific amount of time to share their thoughts, uninterrupted, in turn. Designating a portion of your meetings for employees to share their ideas, thoughts, and feelings without interjection can be a powerful way to make them feel more seen and heard. I've experienced being in faculty meetings and being interrupted by other faculty members. Because I've always been a "junior" faculty member—considered "newer" to the university than my colleagues—and I've always been the only Black woman in those meetings, sometimes I'm ignored or talked over. Providing each individual in the meeting with the opportunity to share is one way to be more inclusive to those whose voices get pushed to the back, stifled, or silenced.

In my classrooms, every semester I always find that some students are much more outspoken than others. Sometimes it's to the point where these more outspoken students are interrupting and talking over others. I've started to be more intentional about circling back to the students who are ignored or talked over and amplifying their thoughts. I also try to call on the students who may be quieter and more introverted but seem like they have a thought they'd like to contribute. When you're leading a meeting, that sort of intentionality is vital and requires first getting to know the employees on your team and then purposefully pulling things out of them during meetings. The round robin technique is a great starting point to decentering white voices in your workplace.

How White Experiences Are Centered

Within society, white voices are centered in too many ways to count. Within Hollywood, for example, the awards given to musicians, actors, and other public figures were created by white people but are also judged based on a white measuring stick. The individuals that decide who is "worthy" of an award are white people. Even the people crafting the "diverse stories" that we love so much are usually those from outside the cultures that the stories represent. I remember talking with my students about the Academy Awards and which actors and movies end up winning. Typically, if a Black actor wins an Oscar, it's for playing in a movie where they reinforced problematic stereotypes about Black people. Halle Berry and Denzel Washington are great examples. I remember Berry's historic win because she was the first Black woman, and is currently the only Black woman, to win the Best Actress award at the Oscars. She won for her role in the film *Monster's Ball*, where she played into the Jezebel stereotype that depicts Black women as hypersexual. In the movie *Training Day*, Denzel Washington won the Best Actor Oscar for playing a crooked detective who engages in corrupt behavior.

Although both movies were good, I felt like Berry and Washington were rewarded only for playing into the negative stereotypes about Black people at a time when the world needed to see more uplifting Black characters. Enslavement narratives and white savior films, in particular—where a white character is "saving" a non-white character (examples include *District 9*, *Avatar*, *Grand Torino*, and *Remember the Titans*)—are what Hollywood typically rewards. Within the last few years, that has started to change, but we see it replicated outside of Hollywood.

In our everyday lives, white voices are centered and rewarded in a myriad of ways. Like the movies, workplaces have several awards they can be nominated for, such as the "Best Places to Work" honors and lists. What I routinely notice when I check which companies have won these awards is the vague criteria being used to judge organizations and institutions. I've had friends who've worked at the companies that are nominated or voted as best companies to work for, and there's a common perception that those lists are BS. I've even heard whispers that some companies pay for these types of designations, awards, and recognition. I'm not sure how true that is, but I don't think it's outside the realm of possibilities. When we think of what makes a place the "best to work for," we're thinking about the white-dominant culture and not about what factors make the workplace an inclusive place for non-white employees.

The criteria used to determine the "best" are based on a white measuring stick. A *New York Times* article from September 2022 reported on the criticism of the US News college rankings and indicated that many of the colleges and universities "reward wealth and white institutions."[5] When we rate what makes a company good to work for, often we're not considering the experiences of non-white employees. Many of the companies that make these lists have engaged in known racist practices. If a company has all of these "amazing" qualities but makes no effort to recruit racially diverse employees and has structures and systems in place that continue the oppression of marginalized employees, how could it possibly be considered one of the "best places to work"? The question that should be asked is: The best place to work for *whom*? One of the ways we prioritize and center whiteness is when it comes to employee experiences. We always hear white voices the loudest, and white voices and white experiences hold much more weight and clout than the experiences of non-white employees.

There have been a lot of critiques of DEI trainings, with many factions claiming that unconscious bias trainings and DEI trainings are largely ineffective. What's so interesting about these critiques is that when you peel back the layers, the "failure" of these trainings is based on perceptions of white employees. If white employees weren't "moved" to change their racist behaviors and racist ideologies, we assume that this type of intervention was unsuccessful. But what about how these types of workshops and trainings make your non-white employees feel? I wrote about this topic in detail for a *Forbes* article, in which I explained that

> the idea that DEI trainings lack utility is predicated on the belief that the sole purpose of these types of trainings is behavior change; and more specifically, behavior change of white people ... more research must explore how DEI trainings make

marginalized employees feel. If there is a possibility that [DEI training] makes marginalized and historically excluded employees feel a greater sense of belonging, inclusion, and equity, why do we continue to disparage and denigrate it?[6]

In the case of workplace DEI trainings (along with virtually every other aspect of our workplace culture), white opinions hold the most weight. It is important to interrogate our perceptions of our workplace DEI interventions to assess whether we are demonizing them based on our own internal white measuring stick.

Racial Gaslighting

In my second book, *The Pink Elephant*, I spoke about *racial gaslighting*, which is when a person from a racially marginalized background shares an experience they've had with racism and their experiences are questioned and invalidated by others.[7] When sharing their workplace experiences, employees from racially marginalized backgrounds may face both racial gaslighting and tone policing (discussed next). Racial gaslighting is one of the reasons why non-white employees may be reluctant to voice their experiences with racism. I've experienced it at different points in my life, much of it while I was in school, since I was in school in mostly white settings for close to three decades of my life. I remember feeling like I was being treated differently at times in my schooling, and when I would bring up the differential treatment I experienced, sometimes others would point to other Black folks who were excelling and not having any issues. That was used as an excuse for why my particular experience was somehow an aberration or a deviation from the norm. I would hear things like, "But so-and-so is on this same team with you and they're doing well. So, that must mean the racism and anti-blackness that you speak of doesn't exist." This was never *verbalized* to me, but these were the sentiments that were being expressed. It seems like the presence of other Black folks thriving somehow negates or invalidates another Black person's experiences with racism and anti-blackness.

Tone Policing

Tone policing occurs when someone is sharing something and the person on the receiving end tries to control or police the manner in which the information is shared. Women and especially non-white women are tone-policed during conversations. Telling someone to "calm down" or saying things like, "It's not that serious" when they're simply expressing some sort of emotion are common forms of tone policing. Advising a person to reframe or rephrase their message based on the emotion that accompanies it is a classic form of tone policing. The fact that tone policing happens more to non-white employees is a prime example of how white voices are centered in the workplace.

I experience tone policing a lot. I come from a family that is naturally loud. My partner always asks me why I'm yelling because I often don't realize my volume; I'm so passionate in the way that I speak. I've engaged in several discussions with people who have told me to "calm down" or "take a chill pill" because they assume from my tone that I'm angry or emotional. Years ago, when I was in graduate school, I lived in a house with several other people. I was talking with one of my roommates-turned-friends (who, for context, is Mexican) and another roommate (who was white) came down to complain about our volume and how our conversation was disturbing his studies. I remember him making a statement that I will never forget, that my roommate-turned-friend and I still joke about to this day: he said I was "naturally loud." I didn't think much of that comment, but my other roommate thought that the statement was racially motivated.

I am assertive and direct in the way I speak, and because of that, I am overly mindful of my tone, especially when engaging in conversations with white people. I'm hyper-aware that I'm loud and I never want my volume to discredit my message or be misconstrued as me being "overly emotional." There are so many ways I realize that I've coddled and centered whiteness, white people, and white voices and modeled my own behaviors in the image of whiteness in my life. Later in the book, I will unpack that in more detail.

Another way that white voices are centered is when it comes to DEI interventions and initiatives. As I mentioned before, sometimes when I work with clients, they think they know what's best, even though I'm being brought in as a subject-matter expert and PhD-trained organizational psychologist. This phenomenon often presents itself when I work with white clients. Some feel that although they value and respect what I'm bringing to the table, ultimately they know what their minoritized and marginalized employees want and need better than I do.

When I start working with a client, the process is typically this: The client (or a representative of the client's) reaches out to me via email to inquire about my DEI consulting services. We schedule a discovery call to discuss their specific needs. If there's alignment, I send a proposal that outlines what a partnership could look like. What's often so interesting is that during the "discovery" phase when I'm on a call with these leaders and ask them probing questions to uncover their specific issues, the leaders have a different perspective of what the issues are compared to when I speak with the employees, especially those from marginalized backgrounds. At the end of the day, the white leaders think that they're omniscient and omnipotent regarding their employees and what's best for the organization, but the process should be more collaborative between leadership and the consultants asked to come in and help.

Decentering White Experiences

It's important to also be intentional about including marginalized voices in panels, focus groups, and qualitative research. In the next chapter, we'll focus on whiteness and how it is centered within the DEI and anti-racism space. But outside of that space, look at and assess who you're bringing in to learn from. Often, the only time we think of non-white people as experts is when they're educating us on topics related to racism and discrimination. I would argue that even *then*, we don't see racially marginalized people as experts of our own oppression. Assess who is allocated to projects, tasks, and assignments at work. I once did some equity work with a TV production company, and one of the issues that came up was that some employees felt they were disproportionately being given assignments and tasks related to their racial/ethnic group. While some employees didn't mind this, there was an overall sentiment of feeling tokenized. Some employees felt like they had to be "representatives" for their community, whereas their white counterparts weren't put in that position. While I do believe in the importance of people being able to speak on behalf of their own communities (Hollywood is a great example of why this is needed, because white creators are often telling the stories of racially marginalized communities), it's important to remember that groups of people are not monolithic. We must see people outside of the racial and ethnic boxes they occupy and not assume that a marginalized employee's sole purpose is to speak "on behalf of" their community.

Think about this question: Does every employee have an equal opportunity to complete projects, tasks, and assignments? It's vital not to adopt a one-size-fits-all management style, even for employees from the same racial and ethnic group. When it comes to white employees, we allow and recognize a plethora of differences and nuance with their individual experiences. We don't afford non-white communities this same sense of diversification. One of the ways that whiteness operates is by us making it the norm and considering everything else as "other." Non-white groups are often seen as one. Even my use of the term *non-white* throughout this book seemingly lumps all non-white people together. (For convenience I prefer the catch-all term *non-white* to listing racial and ethnic groups hundreds of times throughout this book.) Black people, for example, are assumed to have the same experiences, yet we allow white people to be viewed through different and varying lenses. Reanalyze how you allocate work in your workplace. Assess whether there are better ways to allot job assignments, tasks, and projects and whether your workplace system shows preference to white employees (spoiler alert: it does).

Disaggregate Survey Data

When I start consulting with a new client, I often ask for employee data to get a better understanding of the work environment. Sometimes clients can't disclose this information to me, but they can give me a general understanding of the hiring and retention rates. For smaller organizations, I find that this information is tracked less. As the popular saying goes, "What gets measured gets improved." It's important not only to collect this data but also to separate it out so that you can assess recruitment and retention for different underrepresented racial groups. What I often find is that there's a general sense of recruitment and retention data collectively, but there isn't always a clear picture of these statistics when it comes to different groups of employees. Outside of the US, Canada, and the UK there may be countrywide restrictions on collecting racial and ethnic data.[8] It's challenging to design interventions to address the recruitment and retention of employees from underrepresented racial groups if you're not asking employees about their race or ethnicity. Again, how can you improve what you don't measure?

It's important first to collect that data in your workplace and second to figure out your recruitment and retention rates. If you live in a place where asking for racial and ethnic data is prohibited, you can do your own data collection based on what you know about your employees and how you think they may identify. Of course, this isn't a foolproof method if you're guessing; race is tricky because it's a socially created construct, and there are a lot of gray areas. Your guesses about people's racial and ethnic categories may not be perfect, but you're taking a step in the right direction by at least trying to evaluate this. Make sure you're disaggregating your data to better understand recruitment and retention figures.

For smaller organizations where there are only a few employees from underrepresented racial groups, getting feedback from underrepresented employees can be more challenging. One of my clients, for example, is a small company with only about two hundred employees. When the company has sent out surveys through its third-party survey tool, it's been unable to obtain rich racial and ethnic data because there were so few employees from underrepresented racial groups willing to share this information. There may have been fears of "outing" oneself by revealing racial and ethnic identity in such a homogenous workplace. For small companies, nonprofits, and universities: if you have only a few employees from underrepresented racial groups, I suggest using your resources to hire an outside firm or consultant to collect qualitative data and assess employee feedback. Employees can sometimes feel like their HR department is working on behalf of the workplace and not on behalf of the employee. I find that employees feel safer with me as an external or outside entity.

One of the services I provide my clients with is qualitative data analyses. This involves having multiple conversations with employees on a DEI council, in an affinity or employee resource group, or with employees who volunteer to share their feedback. I have a series of questions I ask to assess employees' feelings around the culture of equity and inclusion and then I develop a detailed report based on my findings from these confidential conversations. As an external consultant, I try to do as much as I can to mask the qualitative data and not reveal the identity of the employees who are sharing while still providing stakeholders with trends and patterns that I notice through the qualitative analysis. Utilizing an outside firm or consultant to assess patterns and trends among different racial groups can be an effective strategy if your workplace lacks racial or ethnic diversity.

Analyze Exit Interview Data

One way to decenter white voices in the workplace is to analyze nonwhite employee experiences to understand what is leading them to exit your workplace. It's vital not only to collect exit information when employees leave the workplace, but also to disaggregate that data. A few clients I've seen conduct both an exit survey and an exit interview. I always think it's best to collect as much data as you can or as much data as employees are willing to share. There are a few different types of exit information you can collect from employees: an exit survey, an actual exit interview with an HR professional or workplace representative, or resignation emails and physical letters.

I've never completed an exit interview before leaving a job except for one of my jobs during graduate school, when I worked as a bank teller. I was fed up with the working conditions and even though I'd told my manager I could work only thirty hours or less, I was routinely being scheduled for forty-plus hours with lots of overtime, and the bank branch was perpetually understaffed. In my frustration, I submitted my resignation letter one day before I planned to leave. I know that the standard is to give a two-week notice, but cut me a little slack for being a very frustrated twenty-something. I handed my letter in on a Thursday afternoon with the intent to leave by the end of day Friday. My boss passed the letter on to the assistant branch manager, who called me into her office to ask me why I was quitting. It was a bit of an informal exit interview, but I was kind of nervous to share my entire experience with her, which is why I wrote a detailed letter outlining my feelings and reasons for leaving. Situations like this are why it's crucial to disaggregate employee exit information to decenter white employee voices and experiences in your workplace.

6

decentering whiteness in the dei and anti-oppression space

One of the most insidious and pervasive ways that whiteness is centered is within DEI spaces. The white-centering that occurs there is much more difficult to spot and address. DEI practitioners, activists, and those who work within the anti-oppression space are considered experts and leaders, and others look to us for guidance and direction. For this reason, we are less likely to be held to the same standards as other people when it comes to our own biases. The perception is that we "know better" and "do better," so the public may be less likely to criticize us. Those of us who do anti-oppression work may also be less likely to engage in the self-reflection that is necessary for growth, development, and evolution. Because we are seen as experts and leaders in this domain, it's easy to develop an ego that prevents us from being introspective, self-aware, and self-reflective.

White-Centering in the Anti-oppression Space

According to data compiled by Zippia.com from 2010 to 2019, 76 percent of chief diversity officers in the US are white.[1] Although this number doesn't reflect all the folks who do DEI-related work, the executive-level DEI positions that come with greater pay and more power to influence the workplace are overwhelmingly white. Within the DEI and anti-oppression space, white people and white-adjacent folks are prioritized. In this context, when I say "white-adjacent," I'm referring to someone from a racially marginalized background who aligns themselves with whiteness and distances themselves from their own racial or ethnic group. Many times, people manipulate their appearance to gain more access to the privileges that come with being white. An example might be someone who racially appears white but ethnically is Persian and denounces their Persian background so as to not experience bias, or a white Latina who dyes her hair blonde to appear more white. Because we all understand how whiteness works and how it is prioritized and centered within society, many non-white folks strategically strive for white-adjacency and may alter their looks to appear closer to white.

In addition, an alarming number of white-led DEI businesses have received venture capital funding and resources compared with DEI companies created by non-white people.[2] I saw this happen within a university I worked in years ago. Upon realizing that it had several issues with racial inequity, the university hired a white-led DEI firm to help remedy the problem. It was so off-putting that the university administrators didn't even realize how problematic it was to hire a white firm to help them with issues of racism. As many books as white practitioners have read, lacking the lived experiences of racism limits their ability to help address issues of systemic racism. That situation for me was just another cruel reminder of how whiteness is centered even in the spaces that were designed to dismantle it.

It's not just white people. I recognize that I'm more palatable to employers as a DEI consultant because I'm lighter-skinned, have green eyes, and have a PhD. Colorism, featurism, and elitism provide me with privileges that many of my counterparts do not possess. Lighter-skinned people of *any* racial or ethnic group are thrust to the forefront of many of the movements that have catalyzed the world. One thing I noticed during the post–George Floyd era of 2020 was that many of the activists and social justice folks that went viral and received heightened notoriety were either white or had some proximity to whiteness. Some of our favorite Black activists have white proximity through their light skin. In 2020 and beyond, many of the social media accounts people flocked to for anti-racism learning and education and many of the most prominent anti-racism authors, writers, and thought leaders in the space are those who are white, white adjacent, or have white proximity.

White DEI and anti-racism practitioners are prioritized more on social media. When perusing social media influencers that speak about anti-racism and racial justice, I've found that many of the ones with the largest followings are the white "educators." The world loves to give white people cookies, as my friend and fellow DEI practitioner Joquina Reed says, just for doing the bare minimum. A form of digital blackface is also a growing problem I've noticed on social media, manifested as white creators who construct their social media pages in a way that makes their audience assume or think they're Black.

The ever-evolving nature of society has also prompted some white people to manipulate their appearance to gain more access to opportunities that may come from being seen as Black, a phenomenon known as *blackfishing*. A classic example of this is Rachel Dolezal, a former NAACP chapter president who was posing as a Black woman until 2015, when it was revealed that she was white.[3] Jessica Krug is another example. Krug was a Black studies professor who made a blog post in 2020 admitting that she'd spent her career posing as a Black woman.[4] Following Dolezal's case, there have been a slew of other white women posing as non-white for material gain.

We're also seeing what could be thought of as mixed-fishing or race-fishing, where white people trick the public into believing they are non-white in order to gain access, clout, and notoriety. The most recent example is the story of Raquel Evita Saraswati, who misrepresented herself as being of Arab, Latine, and South Asian heritage. Saraswati served as a diversity executive and spokesperson for Muslim and LGBTQ issues, but in early 2023 it was revealed that she was white.[5] When the spotlight isn't on a white person, many white people feel an inherent desire to do anything possible to recenter themselves; even when it comes to experiences of oppression that they've never endured. White voices never want to be excluded from the conversation.

Being "woke" is profitable, and the most sought-after resource in today's world is attention. People will steal content and creations from those who are doing the work to change oppressive systems, in an attempt to "go viral" and achieve short-lived fame and notoriety. There is also a pattern within society of praising white people who speak out against racism more than those with lived experiences of racism. We somehow find racial justice conversations sexier and more appealing when it's coming from the mouth of a white person. Many of us, myself included, have held onto the belief that "white ice is colder."

As mentioned, in the summer of 2020 when the world was flocking to anti-racist literature to help expand their consciousness, many of the most prominent voices were white. Robin DiAngelo, for example, has been a prominent figure in the DEI and anti-racism space because of her *New York Times* best-selling book *White Fragility*. I am ashamed to say I listened to the audiobook version when it first came out, without realizing how problematic it was. When reviewing the DEI-related books I purchased when I started my consultancy five years ago, I found that all of them were written by white authors. Some of the authors on my bookshelf at the time included Heather Mac Donald, Howard J. Ross, Jennifer Brown, and Tim Wise. I held on tightly to a misguided belief that white authors could teach me more about bias and oppression than what I had experienced as a Black woman living in America. Many of us don't even stop to think about the absurdity of us flocking to white people to teach us about something they've never personally experienced. The irony of me seeking out white people to teach me about something I have lived and learned is simply mind-blowing.

White expertise is *always* prioritized over lived experience. To paraphrase what I've written in the past, non-white people aren't even seen as experts of our own oppression.

Jane Elliott is a white, ninety-year-old educator who made waves when she did a Blue Eyes/Brown Eyes exercise in 1968. To many, Elliott is considered one of the founders of diversity training and an expert in the field. I remember when a producer for a popular daytime talk show reached out to me for a series of racial equity workshops. I was so excited about the workshops because the show was one that my mom watched daily. When I had an initial conversation with the producer, they asked if I was familiar with Elliott's Blue Eyes/Brown Eyes exercise and if I could do it or something similar in the workshop. I was familiar with the exercise, but was a bit annoyed that I was being asked to replicate it. Despite my somewhat positive feelings about Elliott, I remember thinking how preposterous it was for me to replicate her exercise in my own racial equity workshops. As well received as that exercise may have been when Elliott conducted it (likely due to the fact that she is white), I felt insulted by the ask, as if somehow Elliott knew more about teaching people about racism than me, a person living in a Black body that experiences racism and anti-blackness on a consistent basis. It didn't matter that I was a PhD-trained organizational psychologist, or that my dissertation focused on bias. My knowledge, skills, expertise, and lived experience didn't matter.

Fast-forward to when I had an opportunity to meet Jane Elliott in person in 2019. If you scroll far enough back on my Instagram page, you'll see a picture I took with her. It was interesting to witness a live workshop of hers, but there was one part of the workshop I didn't enjoy. She asked the mostly white audience whether any of them would want to be a Black person for a day. I thought it was an odd question with an obvious enough answer. It seemed from my perspective that the main focus of her training session was to somehow induce empathy from her audience by encouraging them to put themselves in the shoes of Black people. But there was zero consideration for how that question made me, as a Black person, or the other Black people in the audience feel. I felt degraded, as if somehow my life wasn't valuable because no white person wanted to trade places with me. Non-white people often become the sacrificial lambs in DEI workshops and trainings. White enlightenment always comes at the expense of racially marginalized people.

In reflecting on Elliott's workshop from years ago, I think what made me so uncomfortable was the idea that empathy would somehow decrease systemic racism. I am a firm believer that empathy is *not* effective in changing oppressive systems. I know that empathy is often touted as the cure-all for racism. In my lifetime, I've seen Black bodies being brutalized and no amount of empathy has introduced specific and tangible policies to protect Black people from harm. If the videotapes of Rodney King's beating, George Floyd's killing, and the brutality against Tyre Nichols didn't make white people feel empathy, why do we focus so much on empathy in our anti-racism efforts? Later on in the book, we'll dive more into why empathy is often an exercise in white-centering.

Centering White Comfort

Another way that whiteness is centered in the DEI and anti-oppression space is the centering of white feelings. When DEI practitioners are developing interventions to address the needs of an organization or institution, we have conversations with leadership, who are often white. White leaders will share their needs, wants, and desires, and we, as practitioners, are expected to cater to these needs. I remember the numerous times I centered white feelings when I started consulting. There is one conversation in particular that I will never forget. A company had reached out to me pre-pandemic for a workshop. Usually when someone reaches out to me to inquire about consulting or a workshop, I schedule a discovery call with them to learn more about their specific needs. On this particular call, a white leader was explaining the issues that her company was facing and how education was a huge hurdle the company had to overcome to create a more inclusive environment for all employees. After I shared with her the structure and style of my awareness workshops, she specifically asked about topics and proceeded to list topics and titles she wanted to stay away from. She told me she wanted to make sure that if she hired me to facilitate a workshop I'd stay away from discussing "controversial topics" like white privilege and white supremacy. Though I was a bit flummoxed by this request at the time, I agreed to avoid those topics so I could win her business. I didn't fully realize the gravity of this decision and other decisions I had been making to prioritize whiteness within my own DEI consultancy.

In September 2020, the Trump administration announced that all federal agencies that were receiving diversity training had to ensure it did not focus on critical race theory.[6] Teaching or training in a way that focused on systemic racism, and the role that white-centering and white supremacy have played in continuing oppression, was now prohibited. A few clients reached out to me about my educational content and how to ensure that it was compliant with these new regulations. When Trump lost the 2020 presidential election, these new restrictions never came to fruition. There was little discussion around the problematic nature of prioritizing white comfort over the feelings of the racially oppressed. At that point in my journey, I wasn't willing to comply with the mandates had they gone into effect. I had already told myself that if I was working with an organization or institution that wanted me to remove discussions about systemic racism from my workshops, I would decline that partnership. I have come a long way from the days I centered and prioritized whiteness in my work. At some point a few years ago, I had a realization: centering whiteness was not going to be what liberated the most marginalized people.

In the fall of 2022, the world was grappling with the death of Queen Elizabeth II. The chatter on LinkedIn was quite interesting. Many people from countries that were colonized by the British expressed their disdain for the queen and the British monarchy. But there was also much criticism hurled at those who weren't expressing sadness over her passing. This is a prime example of how workplace conversations don't allow employees to express "contrarian" views about the white-dominant populations that have caused harm to marginalized communities. When it comes to topics that are seen as "off-limits" in the workplace, white comfort is always prioritized. Within the workplace, we center white comfort in a number of ways that we probably don't even realize, such as:

- Shutting down discussions around topics that make white people feel uncomfortable. This can include but is not limited to discussions about systemic racism, white supremacy, white domestic terrorism, and white anger, described by *White Rage* author Carol Anderson as the negative response white people have to topics of structural and systemic racism.[7] White rage and white tears are often used as tools to derail conversations about race and avoid accountability for committing racial harms.

- Expecting non-white employees to contort themselves to appease white customers. This can include overt actions like asking a Black employee to wear their hair in more Eurocentric or "professional" ways, or it could be more subconscious or unconscious. Employees may be offered classes to "refine" their speech, which sends the message that they should *code-switch*, or change the way they speak to mimic the vernacular of the white-dominant culture

- In her best-selling book, *The Memo*, Minda Harts talks about a manager that made a comment about her bright orange nails.[8] Making snide or microaggressive comments about an aspect of an individual's physical appearance sends the message that they must alter themselves in order to be more acceptable and professional.

Our whole conception of professionalism is based on white ideals. Non-white employees are sent constant messages that in order to ascend, they must align themselves to whiteness as much as possible. Later in the book, we'll discuss how racially marginalized communities learn to prioritize and center whiteness.

White-Centering in DEI Messaging

For individuals who work as DEI trainers, workshop facilitators, and speakers, our content is often very white-centric. When I first started my consultancy, I was mainly being hired by organizations and institutions to facilitate workshops and training sessions. Aside from the fact that I centered my workshop content on what I felt would make white employees and leaders feel most comfortable, white-centering was showing up even within my messaging, content, and imagery. I was overly mindful of the words I was using on my website so as to not anger my mostly white audiences. I now realize how much I was prioritizing whiteness in my business.

Analyzing my workshops and trainings specifically, I recognize that I prioritized and centered whiteness by 1) centering the needs of white leaders and white comfort, and 2) using images of white people in workshops and training sessions. We've explored the first point in this chapter, but it wasn't until the last few years that I recognized how problematic the second point was, where I was subconsciously and unconsciously using *only* images of white people in my stock photos. I would often use white people in the PowerPoint slides I created for workshops because those images were easier to find. I recognize now that there was a subconscious component to it as well. I knew that white people would feel more comfortable seeing images of people that looked like them, and I thought making white people comfortable was the goal in the workshops and training sessions I was facilitating.

White-Centering in DEI Strategy and Consulting Work

For individuals who work as consultants and DEI strategists, there are several ways that we knowingly and unknowingly center whiteness in our work. Our desire to cater to what white leaders want when they hire us as the subject-matter experts is one example. Now, those of you who are DEI practitioners might be reading this and wondering, *If we don't cater to the needs of white leaders, won't we be out of a job?* That's a valid question. But we must go into this work understanding that our ultimate and true goal should be to make our jobs obsolete. In an ideal world, none of us would be doing this work. I recognize that there is still *so much* work to be done, but I wish and hope that one day my job won't be needed. Every company is at a different level in its learning and development, but any organization or institution that is *not* willing to decenter whiteness will continue to be plagued with issues of racism, oppression, and injustice.

Employee resource groups and workplace affinity groups are a great case study. As we saw in chapter 5, in some organizations, these groups—originally designed to be safe spaces for people with a shared characteristic or identity— have become open to *all* employees. In other words, a community that was created as a safe space for those with a particular marginalized identity has been infiltrated by "allies" and aspiring allies. I've heard the narrative before that allowing others to join ERGs and affinity groups gives these groups a sense of legitimacy. But what are we really saying? That groups within our workplace are not legitimate unless white people cosign them? Even within the specific interventions that are designed to create more equity and justice, white-centering prevails.

Another workplace intervention aimed at racial equity that often diverts to white-centering behaviors is mentorship and sponsorship programs, which are often used to improve retention of employees from underrepresented racial groups. Within these types of programs, typically white leaders are put in positions to guide and advocate for junior employees from underrepresented racial groups. This type of dynamic promotes the *white savior complex*, the ideology that non-white people need to be saved, taught, and helped by white people who are ultimately all-knowing. There's not enough conversation about how these types of workplace relationships, which were originally created to help underrepresented employees ascend, become a perverse tool to center whiteness.

A few years ago, I realized that I had prioritized and centered whiteness in what I chose to name my DEI consultancy: BWG Business Solutions. BWG stands for "black white green." The idea behind this is something I used to say, "Diversity is not about black or white but green," meaning that prioritizing DEI will allow a workplace to be sustainable and remain revenue-generating. In naming my consultancy this, I initially wanted to appeal to white leaders, who at the time didn't have a clear conception of the "value" or "business case" for prioritizing DEI. In 2023 and beyond, we are past the point of having to convince white leaders about the value of this work. Coddling white feelings and catering to whiteness will not move us closer to liberation.

Decentering Whiteness in DEI Consulting Work

As I've stated, when I started my consultancy, I focused on appeasing white leaders. I figured that doing what they wanted would mean happier leaders and thus happier workplaces, but it's often the opposite. Doing what leaders want means I'm prioritizing the needs of these white people over racially marginalized employees. We, as anti-oppression practitioners, *must* center our work around these two questions: 1) Who are the most marginalized employees in the workplace? 2) What do *they* need to feel safe, supported, and prioritized? Think about whose voice is the loudest in your workplaces and how to center the voices of the most vulnerable. For example, when surveys are being conducted to assess the employee experience, disaggregate the data so you can get a snapshot of the specific experiences of different groups of employees. Who is leading the company's DEI efforts? Are these efforts also focused on anti-racism? An interesting thing I noticed when I started my consultancy is that *DEI* is seen as an umbrella term, but few companies are actually making concerted efforts to advance racial equity specifically. Look at what DEI initiatives and programs are being pushed forward in your workplace. Are they targeted at helping to grow, develop, and promote the most marginalized? Are they focused on marginalized identities that are seen as "safer"? In both the work that I do and my personal experiences, I find that those of us who speak specifically about racism and anti-blackness experience a great deal of pushback compared to DEI practitioners that focus on topics like gender equity, psychological safety, and neurodiversity. There is less apprehension about conversations on these topics than conversations centered on how whiteness and white culture is destructive and harmful. Think about what DEI efforts are given credence, support, and priority. Oftentimes even *within* your DEI efforts and interventions, there is a hierarchy and certain initiatives are given more priority over others.

I'll say it again: operating in a way that prioritizes white comfort will not lead to Black liberation or the liberation of any other oppressed and marginalized group. I have thought about changing my company name, but decided to leave it. I do believe that prioritizing diversity, equity, inclusion, belonging, and justice will move the workplace closer to liberation and this will help an organization remain profitable. I still believe the wealth of evidence indicating that racial and ethnic diversity is beneficial for a number of reasons, one of which is profitability, but beyond that, younger generations of workers are demanding representation, equity, accessibility, and justice. Any workplace that neglects these needs not only will lose money but also won't be sustainable in the future. I'm not proud of where I started from, but we all have space for continuous growth and evolution. I like to keep my business's name also as a way to prove to others that even though some people may see me as an "expert" or "thought leader" in the DEI space, I have and continue to make mistakes and errors, and I am continuously growing, learning, and evolving.

White-Centering When Sourcing Vendors and Independent Contractors

When sourcing outside entities like consultants, practitioners, trainers, and speakers, companies operate from a white-centric lens. In general, we are more likely to think of white people as experts than non-white individuals. I've experienced this many times, when I would tell people I was an educator and they would assume I was a K–12 teacher. The assumption is that I could not be a professor. And when I would say that I was a college professor, people would assume I was an adjunct professor. The shock on people's faces when I explained that I was a full-time assistant professor was always hilarious. Although I hold a PhD, my knowledge, skills, and expertise are constantly questioned and undermined.

When organizations and institutions are seeking to partner with external consultancies, I find that often by default, the companies they choose to work with and purchase goods and services from are white-owned and white-led businesses. As I mentioned earlier, when the university I worked in decided it needed the help of external DEI consultants to remedy its equity issues, it hired a white-led DEI consultancy. In my experiences, many of the pervasive issues in the university were related to racism and racial inequities, so when I received an email about the university's new partnership with this DEI consultancy, I was interested to learn more about who it had hired to help with its equity efforts. After doing some digging, I found out that it was a white-owned DEI consultancy. Again, this is a classic example of white-centering.

Workplaces are more likely to lean on white vendors and independent contractors and don't often realize that this is due to our unconscious biases and our ingrained need to center whiteness. We often associate non-white businesses as being "less than" and not as high-quality as white-owned businesses. This is a familiar trend, particularly when it comes to Black-owned businesses. Within the Black community, although many of us want to support Black-owned businesses, unconsciously and subconsciously we're sometimes reticent and hesitant to support them. Anyone that knows me knows how much I love Black-owned businesses. On my Instagram page, I have two different Instagram story highlights that showcase videos and images of Black-owned businesses that my followers should support. I've always made a concerted effort to shop and buy Black as much as possible, but there have been times that I, too, have questioned the quality of the product or service I would be receiving from a Black-owned businesses. I've found myself jumping to conclusions and assuming the worst from Black-owned businesses I was patronizing, and I've had to check myself. That anti-blackness is ingrained so deeply within all of us—even those of us who are Black.

Decentering Whiteness When Sourcing Vendors and Independent Contractors

Decentering whiteness when it comes to sourcing vendors and independent contractors means recognizing that the propensity to center whiteness exists and then making a specific effort to source vendors and contractors that are Black, Indigenous, Asian, Latine, Middle Eastern, Pacific Islander, and so on. Develop or utilize a list of vendors and independent contractors from underrepresented populations. Following the murder of George Floyd, when there was an increased interest in finding Black anti-racism educators and consultants, Awaken founder and CEO Michelle Kim developed a list of Black anti-racism consultants that companies can hire.[9] What's stopping *you* from creating your own list? This could be something as simple as a Google form you send out and encourage employees to share too. This will help you generate your own database that you can refer back to when sourcing vendors. You can also utilize word-of-mouth channels and put out a call to your networks and communities that you're looking for vendors from underrepresented and underserved communities. Hold yourself accountable as a workplace, and every year review the vendors and independent contractors that you've employed. Strive to increase this number each year and think about sharing this number with your employees.

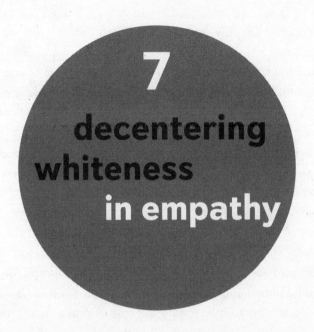

7

decentering whiteness in empathy

After the murder of George Floyd, there were a plethora of think pieces centered on racial equity and anti-racist practices in different industries. In much of the conversations around racial equity, empathy was one of the ingredients that was encouraged. When I search the words *empathy* and *racism*, 14 million search results come up. *Empathy* is defined by *Merriam-Webster* Online as "the action of understanding, being aware of, being sensitive to, and vicariously experiencing the feelings, thoughts, and experience of another of either the past or present without having the feelings, thoughts, and experience fully communicated in an objectively explicit manner."[1] Much of the discussion suggests an inverse relationship between empathy and prejudice: the more empathy a person has, the less prejudiced they will be. I started to rethink the role of empathy in eradicating racism a few years ago after attending a Jane Elliott workshop. As I mentioned in the previous chapter, Elliott has been an educator for decades and gained prominence with the Blue Eyes/Brown Eyes exercise she created in

1968. Elliott has become a well-known voice when it comes to racial discrimination.

During the workshop when Elliott asked the crowd how many of us would want to be a Black person for a day, I wondered why a question like that had to be asked to see my full humanity. Elliott was trying to make the audience of non-Black people more empathetic to the Black experience, with the idea that it would make them less racist toward us. But racism isn't just ill feelings toward a person based on their race. Racism comprises the systems that exist to subjugate racially marginalized people. A few years ago, *Merriam-Webster* updated its definition of *racism* to include systemic oppression.[2] Trying to elicit empathy by asking the types of questions Elliott asked, which are dehumanizing to Black people, doesn't actually change the systems and structures that continue to harm and oppress Black people. It was then that I started to interrogate the role of empathy in eradicating racism.

I used to be a huge advocate for empathy. In fact, I wrote a piece in 2018 about empathy, calling it "the key to a diverse and inclusive workplace."[3] And while I do believe that empathy has *some* utility, I don't believe it's the key to eradicating racism, as I had previously thought. After the murder of George Floyd, I started to feel uneasy about the idea of empathy and claims that it's the north star to eradicating racism. Does putting ourselves in the shoes of others *really* help us understand other people's experiences and mitigate our biases? I remember growing up and hearing about the Los Angeles riots that happened after the Rodney King verdict. Rodney King was a Black man who was beaten by police officers in 1991 after a high-speed police chase. His beating caused a reverberating impact around the country because this was one of the first times that police brutality was caught on camera in the United States.[4] But since Rodney King, a number of others have experienced police violence that was caught on film. Eric Garner was a Black man whose Staten Island death was recorded in 2014. He was put into an illegal chokehold by an NYPD officer and was heard on camera saying, "I can't breathe."[5]

George Floyd's video sent shock waves around the world, and the fact that the murder happened during the Covid-19 pandemic intensified collective outcry. The horrific murders of these and so many other Black people that have been caught on film has taught me this: body cameras capturing violence and murder do little to make others see Black humanity. The pull of whiteness is so strong that after our initial outrage, it seduces us all into a lull and we forget about the structural and systemic barriers that we were fighting against. Many claim that being able to actually *see* the harm committed against Black people will induce empathy, which will lead to changes. Although those situations may make us more empathetic, that empathy doesn't actually diminish our racist behaviors. And I would argue that it shouldn't take Black death or harm to induce changes. Black pain and trauma are often exploited for public gain with few tangible policies being created to catalyze change.

In my quest to better understand the role of empathy in eradicating racism, I stumbled upon a book written by Yale psychologist Paul Bloom. I remember him from a *20/20* segment that I used to show my students every year in a social psychology class I taught. Bloom wrote the thought-provoking book *Against Empathy*, analyzing the role of empathy in our lives. The book argues that empathy itself is vulnerable to bias. The empathy we feel for another person can vary based on factors such as whether the person is a friend or enemy, whether they are part of our group or an opposing group, and even whether the person is attractive or not.[6]

Our empathy bias has been discussed through various lenses, including the Missing White Woman Syndrome, a term coined by PBS news anchor Gwen Ifill to describe the phenomenon in which the media seems to only care about a missing person when it is a white girl or a white woman.[7] Because of this empathy bias, we care more about the suffering of people who are similar to us. Living in a white-centered society means that we are more interested (oftentimes unconsciously) in the plight of others when they are white. In 2014, the African American Policy Forum (AAPF) spearheaded the Say Her Name movement to raise awareness about the alarming number of Black women and girls who experience police brutality and violence that doesn't receive the same amount of media attention.[8] Other organizations, such as the Black & Missing Foundation, Inc. (BAMFI) and Missing and Murdered Indigenous Women (MMIW), were created to raise awareness about missing and harmed Black and Indigenous populations.

Another flaw of empathy that Bloom cites in his book is the "spotlight effect." Empathy makes us focus on one specific individual or specific event, which can be myopic. It doesn't allow us to look at the bigger picture and recognize how our actions impact groups of people. An excellent example Bloom points to is the reaction to the Sandy Hook tragedy compared to the ongoing violence in Chicago. In the Sandy Hook school shooting, twenty-year-old Adam Lanza took the lives of twenty-eight people, the majority of whom were young children.[9] The shooting, which took place in Newtown, Connecticut, rightfully received a visceral reaction from the public. We haven't seen the same reaction to the situation in Chicago, where more children are murdered on a daily basis. The difference is that those impacted by the tragedy in Newtown were white, whereas the violence taking place in Chicago involves mostly Black people. Even our empathy is white-centered. The public is better able to empathize with the harm that white people experience than any other racial group.

Empathy-inducing activities like Jane Elliott's question don't achieve the goals that we hope they will accomplish; they do nothing to actually reduce our racism. Part of the reason why empathy isn't the silver bullet we want it to be is that our ability to put ourselves in others' shoes is limited by our biases. A related phenomenon that shows up in the workplace, one that I've written about before, is the idea that people from underrepresented racial and ethnic groups should exploit their trauma for the sake of white enlightenment. In a 2021 article for *Forbes*, I questioned whether resharing past experiences with racism will lead to systemic changes. I challenged the notion that empathy is what we should be striving for and what will help us move closer to racial equity.[10]

My issue with the resharing of past traumas is twofold. People from racially marginalized backgrounds are asked to regurgitate past harms and share these experiences with coworkers. It almost feels like a performance: non-white employees performing for white audiences. After the murder of George Floyd, a friend of mine told me that he'd been asked by his organization to talk about a past experience with racism. My friend worked at a large Fortune 100 company, and there may have been hundreds of people present while he gave this talk. I was frustrated because it seemed like his leadership assumed that sharing these experiences was somehow cathartic for him, when in fact the retelling of our past traumas can trigger us and send us back to a place we have healed from or evolved past. It's like a bad breakup. You think you've moved past it and healed from it, but when someone brings that person's name up, having to relive that breakup experience can bring back all those memories and feelings you never wanted to feel again. That's how it can feel for many of us when retelling past experiences with racism.

Employees from underrepresented racial backgrounds are sometimes asked to share these traumas for the sake of white enlightenment and learning. I argue that white enlightenment doesn't have to come at the expense of racially marginalized people. A friend of mine, who is Black, was a DEI consultant who worked for a small boutique consulting firm. She shared with me that she was always the one to facilitate workshops on racism and was encouraged by the other white facilitators to lean on her past experiences with racism. She explained how demoralizing those experiences had started to become. She felt like she was being asked to reshare very painful parts of her past over and over again. At first, she was fine with it because of the money that she was making. But eventually it became too exhausting for her and she eventually quit the job.

Moving Away from Empathy to Decenter Whiteness in Our Workplace

These empathy-inducing activities that we engage in are white-centered. We have to move away from this quest for empathy. Many have theorized that if we focus on empathy and encourage employees to be more empathetic, we'll be able to diminish their prejudice. The problem with this theory is that it simply doesn't hold true, especially in a workplace context. To foster an environment built on equity and justice, we *must* recognize and understand the ways that different communities have been historically marginalized and excluded. This recognition and understanding does not require us to exploit employees' racial trauma and past pain; we have clear examples of the ways that systems have historically marginalized and excluded different populations. This educational understanding will help us to create interventions that rectify these historical harms. When we think objectively about empathy's role in our quest for racial equity, empathy has little utility. Even if employees are able to "put themselves in the shoes of others," dismantling oppression requires systemic change. Empathy is ineffective because it doesn't get at the root problem. Systemic changes are what workplace environments need.

Instead of chasing after empathy or trying to generate more empathy from employees, we can focus on these two strategies instead:

EDUCATE EMPLOYEES When we have a deep understanding of the experiences of others, we're able to better support them. If each employee recognized the impact that Japanese internment or redlining had on different generations and communities, there would be more sensitivity around the needs of different communities. What education can you provide for employees to help them continuously grow and strengthen their awareness and understanding? Think about facilitators, trainers, and educators who can enlighten employees on a number of unique issues and topics. I rarely see workplace discussions on the impacts of war or regional conflict on employees. What is hair discrimination, and how does it impact employees with Afro-textured hair? What is it like to be a caregiver to someone who is terminally ill or has a long-term disability? Think about expanding the typical programming your organization may already have in place. While it's important to know the ABCs of diversity, equity, and inclusion, our learning must expand past that.

ENCOURAGE COMPASSIONATE LISTENING Compassionate listening means hearing what a person is saying without feeling the need to invalidate their experiences. Listen without feeling the need to relate their experience to your own. As I mentioned earlier in the book, a few years ago, my maternal grandmother passed away. When my mom shared with someone that her mother had passed away, they said something along the lines of "I know how you feel." My mom was seething; she told me that person couldn't have had any idea how she was feeling. Also think back to the story I shared at the beginning of this book when I attended the conference and Karen compared having red hair to experiencing Black hair discrimination. Rather than trying to compare an incomparable experience of racism, she should have practiced compassionate listening in that moment.

Ask employees how their past experiences have shaped their current realities. For example, how does student loan debt impact you as an employee? How has generational trauma affected your current experiences? Rather than making empathy the goal and encouraging "walking a mile in someone's moccasins," provide employees with the tools to be more compassionate listeners. When it comes to compassionate listening, it's helpful to remember three Rs: listen without feeling the need to *respond, relate, or provide recommendations*. Think about holding compassionate listening sessions weekly, monthly, or quarterly to provide employees, especially non-white employees, with an opportunity to feel heard without being interrupted or invalidated.

8
decentering whiteness within us

We cannot decenter whiteness in the workplace without recognizing and grappling with the ways we've personally centered whiteness in our own lives. To understand how we can start the process to decenter whiteness within us, I felt it was important and necessary to explain ways that I, even as someone who is writing a book all about decentering whiteness, have struggled with doing so my entire life.

My phenotype, and specifically my hair texture and my lips, is a clear marker that I am "different," and my white peers never let me forget it. When I was maybe nine or ten years old, I would watch my mom wearing different shades of red lipstick and I remember begging her to let me wear some. I think my mom got tired of me begging and let me put on some, and I snuck and wore it to school one day. When I arrived at school, the red lipstick caused quite a stir with my classmates. There were complaints about it, and I think a teacher or an administrator made comments about it. By lunchtime, one of my white classmates asked if

I wanted her help taking it off. I remember my friend commenting about how she didn't understand why people were making such a big deal about the red lipstick when so many other students wore makeup. At that point in my life, I didn't have a conception of racism and didn't realize I was being treated differently because I was one of the only non-white students in the class, and my "big" lips with red lipstick were deemed as "too much."

I remember how much I wanted to alter my lips when I was eleven and twelve years old. I experienced vicious bullying by my British classmates when we were living in Oman and I was attending a British school. While living in the Middle East, I learned that the United States wasn't the only culture that centered whiteness. The size of my lips drew constant commentary from my classmates; they made fun of them to the point where I was eating my lunch in the bathroom to get some relief from their nonstop torment. I remember wondering at the age of twelve whether my parents would let me get lip reduction surgery. (Was that even a thing back then?) I just *knew* that smaller lips would make me "prettier" to my classmates and would maybe stop their jokes. Instead, I transferred to an American school and the harassment stopped.

Our beauty standards have always been based on whiteness. It has definitely been a journey to loving myself and loving my body the way that it was made. My mom has vivid memories of me running in a field outside of our house. I would go out there and practice soccer and sometimes just run. My mom always retells this story and says that I said, "My legs are never going to get big" as I would go outside and run. I had internalized that I needed to be as close as possible to the skinny white woman aesthetic that was popular in the 1990s and early 2000s. Even though researchers have found racial and ethnic variations in body composition, I believed that running would make me skinny like my white classmates.[1] I thought that being as close to white as possible would grant me access into the world of whiteness.

My weight has been a constant source of strife throughout my life. Although I've mostly been on the average to thinner side, my weight has fluctuated my entire life and I never realized how ingrained in me white beauty standards were until I looked back in adulthood. Not only was I constantly running on the field behind our house in fourth and fifth grade so that I could "always be skinny," but throughout school I always played sports (although I wasn't very good at them). I played soccer and basketball, which also involved a lot of running. When I was preparing for junior and senior prom, I started going to the gym with my mom. It's wild to think about being sixteen and seventeen and feeling like I needed to lose weight to look good in my prom dress. No one ever told me that I wasn't fine the way that I was. My parents never said I was fat. But society, and seeing white celebrities and public figures praised for being skinny, made me believe that was what I should be chasing.

When I was playing basketball in middle school, I was one of the few Black kids on the team. My basketball coach made a comment about my body that I will never forget. Although my skin is a lighter shade of brown, my knees and elbows are darker than the rest of my body. One day at basketball practice, my coach asked me why my knees were so dark. I had no response for her. The insinuation felt like an attack. I remember initially feeling like my coach was asking that question to imply something about my actions off the court. I said something along the lines of "they've always been dark," but I was so embarrassed hearing an adult ask me that question. Was something wrong with me and my body? I began to think, "Why are my knees so dark?" Parts of my skin are a different color than other parts because of a common condition known as hyperpigmentation. Black people and those with more melanin in their skin are more susceptible to hyperpigmentation.[2]

At fifteen, I tried SlimFast for the first time. It made my face break out terribly and eventually I had to stop using it. In 2015, I entered my first bodybuilding competition. I went on to participate in three more body-building competitions until I stopped competing in 2018. I think part of my desire to do bodybuilding was rooted in my white-centric idea of what beauty was and how a woman's body should look. I've always been chasing white ideals of beauty, and being skinny was a huge part of that. I took fat burners and water pills designed to make you drop weight quickly. I didn't care as much about the long-term damage those products could do as long as in the short term I achieved the sculpted physique that I thought would help me win the competitions. My desire to chase thinness wasn't the only reason I wanted to start bodybuilding. I love the challenge it required, and as a self-proclaimed foodie, I loved being able to push myself to a level of "skinny" I'd never pushed myself into before. But in reflecting on my decision to start bodybuilding as well as other hobbies I've engaged in throughout my upbringing and even into adulthood, I now realize how many of them were rooted in my innate desire to center whiteness.

My hair has been a huge source of my white-centering behaviors throughout my life. As my sister and I were growing up, my mom had a time trying to figure out how to manage our hair. I have vivid memories of getting chemical straighteners to help manage it until I was an adolescent and my mom went to school for cosmetology. Part of me felt like she went to school solely to learn how to deal with our hair. When she got out of cosmetology school, she was the only one doing our hair. As I entered into my teenage years, I had no desire to wear my hair in the way it naturally grew out of my scalp. I was always made to feel like my hair was unruly and needed to be tamed. When we were in elementary school, there was this white kid—I don't even remember who he was or what he looked like—but whenever he would see us, he would say "cha cha cha chia," the song from the Chia Pets commercial. For those unfamiliar, Chia Pets, terracotta animal figurines that grew chia sprouts to resemble fur or hair, were wildly popular in the 1990s.

It's important while explaining my relationship with my hair to provide some education on the hair typing system. The hair typing system in use today is an iteration of a system that was developed in the early 1900s by Nazi German scientist and known eugenicist Eugen Fischer. As I wrote in a 2022 *Forbes* article about hair discrimination,

> *Fischer used this system in present-day Namibia on the mixed-race population to try and determine "blackness" based on hair texture. Between 1904–1907, Namibia was the site of a mass genocide where German military forces killed approximately 80,000*

of the indigenous Namibian people. This genocide was based on white racial supremacy beliefs. Systems such as the hair typing model developed by Fischer contributed to the subjugation of the Namibian people. Fast forward to today, and Oprah Winfrey's celebrity hair stylist Andre Walker is generally thought of as the person who established and popularized the hair typing system that is currently in use. Based on Walker's method, hair type can be divided into distinct categories based on the texture: 1 is straight hair, 2 is wavy hair, 3 is looser curls, and 4 is considered the coarsest and most tightly curled hair type. Walker's system also associates letters with these numbers to further segment the hair types. Based on the hair typing system, 4c hair is considered to be the kinkiest and most tightly coiled hair texture and by design, the hair texture that experiences the most discrimination.[3]

I have what is considered 4c hair based on the current hair typing system. Although I question whether we should still be using a system that was derived and developed by a known eugenicist, understanding my hair type has been helpful in learning the best practices for taking care of it. It wasn't until the pandemic hit that I had a stark realization about how much white-dominant culture had done a number on me and my perception of self. I never felt like my hair was good enough or beautiful enough because I had been programmed to believe that proximity to whiteness in all aspects of my life is what I should be striving for. Throughout my teenage years, I begged my mom to straighten my hair until eventually she gave in and applied chemical softeners to it to change its texture. I wanted my hair to be straighter and more manageable and I didn't want to be made fun of at school; I wanted to look just like the other white girls. Because I had buried this internalized anti-blackness deep inside myself, it started to manifest in different ways as I entered adulthood.

I stopped getting chemical hair softeners put in my hair in 2012, when I moved to New York for graduate school. I wanted to embrace my natural 4c hair, so I did what's called a Big Chop, where you cut off all the chemically treated hair to start fresh. After doing my Big Chop, I still had some hesitancy about rocking hairstyles that I deemed as "too Black." I worried that I would scare white people and that they would see me in a negative way if I wore hairstyles that were "too Afrocentric" and I didn't want to be seen as too radical. White comfort played a large part in how I styled my hair until just a few years ago.

Because I have what is considered the coarsest and kinkiest hair texture, I've been treated differently than my peers. Years ago, I received a casting email from a popular media site. The email stated that they were looking for hair models for a video campaign and that they wanted to showcase more "diverse" hair textures. I was so excited to read this because at the time, I didn't see a lot of people with my particular hair texture represented in the media. Well, when I scrolled down to the email, it stated that they were looking for type 3 hair only. So, anyone with type 4 hair, like me, was not welcome. The irony was maddening.

White-centering has also manifested for me within the respectability politics that I ascribed to. I was chasing some invisible approval and affirmation from white people. Although I cannot support anything Kanye West does anymore, he says something really poignant in one of his songs, "All Falls Down": "Even if you in a Benz, you still a [n-word] in a coupe." When I heard that line, I knew exactly what he meant. No matter how much money, fame, prestige, accolades, and accomplishments you accumulate, you can never divorce yourself from the anti-blackness that is universal. Growing up, this wasn't a realization I understood. One of the results of my upbringing in primarily white environments was me modeling the behavior I saw displayed by my white peers. Ascribing to respectability showed up in many ways for me.

I used to hate rap music. It's ironic to me now, as a devout trap music enthusiast. I enjoy hearing the poetry these rappers paint of their upbringing and current realities, where they did what they had to do to survive and how they desired for better things than what they ever saw or experienced. When I was younger, though my siblings and even my dad enjoyed rap music, I never liked it. Thinking back now, I recognize that a large part of the reason was because I had somehow internalized the message through the media that rap music was "ghetto." And being called "ghetto" was somehow a slur in my prepubescent mind. I would tell myself that although I was "Black," I wasn't "ghetto," and that brought me relief. I never would have known that in 2023, *ghetto* would be a racial dog whistle and a derogatory term associated with blackness. My anti-blackness ran deep.

My siblings loved one song in particular, "Make 'Em Say Ugh" by rapper Master P. As much as I tried to hate that song, I secretly loved it. Who taught me that Black music was ghetto? It wasn't my family, because they loved and embraced rap music. It wasn't anyone that explicitly told me this. It was a feeling that I got when rap music came on and I saw how white people reacted. It was all the controversy surrounding gangsta rap music in the 1990s. I think I saw all of that and internalized those feelings. *I can't like or listen to rap music because that music makes white people feel uncomfortable,* I would think. So, I stuck to my Jewel, my Alanis Morissette, my Red Hot Chili Peppers, my Avril Lavigne. I would wow my white peers when I knew more about "their music" than many of them. I could list off a number of random facts I learned from VH1's *Pop-Up Video* to impress my classmates. But I had no idea, back then, how I had learned to prioritize and center whiteness even when it came to the music I listened to and promoted.

I am the child of two PhD-trained educators. My father earned a PhD in finance and economics, and my mother earned a PhD in curriculum and instruction. That, coupled with the fact that my parents are West African, meant that education was a huge priority in our household. A lot of West African parents, especially those who immigrate to Western countries, put a huge emphasis on education as a means of upward mobility. For me, college was never a question. It was just a matter of where and what I would study. While I was getting my PhD, I remember reflecting on how much of an emphasis I had placed on education. While I do believe education in whatever form is great and I recommend that every person living on this earth continue learning and educating themselves in different ways, looking back I realize that I did not *need* a PhD. Has it helped me? Absolutely. Did I *need* one to do the work that I am doing now? Not really. This might sound ironic coming from the child of two doctorate-earning parents. I learned that my personal quest for my PhD was because I was chasing some sort of unattainable version of whiteness that I did not realize at the time.

I had equated education with being a more respectable and honorable person, as if somehow I could transcend my blackness if I was educated. I thought a person was more deserving of respect, honor, and dignity based on their education level. My classism was rooted in my desire to attain whiteness. Silly me—I didn't realize that was a futile goal. No matter how much I've accomplished, I still experience anti-blackness and more specifically *misogynoir*, a term coined by Dr. Moya Bailey to describe the unique oppression faced by Black women.

White-centering was also present when I was making a decision for college. My father has taught at a number of historically Black colleges and universities (HBCUs), including Grambling State University, Florida A&M University, Norfolk State University, and Virginia State University. Despite the fact that I could have gone to any of these schools for free because my dad was teaching there, I refused to go. I instead opted for predominantly white institutions (PWIs) for my bachelor's, master's, and doctorate degrees. Now part of me feels disappointed that I never had the "HBCU experience." In undergrad, I attended Virginia Commonwealth University. There were two nearby HBCUs (Virginia Union University and Virginia State University), so I had an opportunity to party with HBCU students, but I never got the full HBCU experience. Looking back, I recognize that my reluctance to attend HBCUs was because of my desire to prioritize whiteness and because of my internalized anti-blackness. I deemed HBCUs as less valuable than PWIs. Who taught me that HBCUs were "less than" PWIs? Society taught me that anything white is right; anything Black, send it back. White-centering played a role not only in my desire to pursue a PhD but also in my choices of college. I ended up saddled with six-figure student loan debt because I was chasing whiteness. I could have had a free ride for my bachelor's degree and my master's degree, but prioritizing whiteness was much more important to me.

While pursuing my PhD, I continued to center whiteness. I started to unplug from the white-centering matrix later in my doctoral program, but when I started it, I was still centering whiteness in many ways. In the beginning, we had to share with our professors what dissertation topics we wanted to focus on so they could assign us a dissertation advisor, a professor who provides guidance, reviews your dissertation at different phases in the writing process, and offers recommendations for refining your dissertation research. For my dissertation, I knew I wanted to expand on a paper about our inherent biases that I had written in a cognitive psychology class while earning my master's degree, with a focus specifically on racial biases. When it was my turn, I shared with my professors and classmates that diversity and inclusion was my area of interest. I was told that none of the professors in the program had a specific focus on diversity and inclusion, but I could be paired with a dissertation advisor from a different university whose research was more aligned with my focus. I agreed to that because I didn't want to be paired with a professor who didn't share my research interests and have to focus on *their* topic of interest for a one-hundred-plus-page dissertation. Then it came time to pitch my dissertation ideas about racial bias in hiring.

My initial dissertation proposal was an idea to study racial differences in hiring, by manipulating LinkedIn profile photos. Although I felt I already knew how the research would go, I was interested in assessing whether race still played a role in a candidate's likelihood to get hired. In 2012, this type of study was much more novel and interesting than it would be now. When I presented that idea, my advisor was on board and we started thinking about how to develop the experiment. But soon my advisor worried that our manipulations would fail and that it would be far too difficult to manipulate the race of the job candidates. We didn't have access to Photoshop, so figuring out how to darken and lighten the skin of the sample job candidates was a bit tricky. I knew my heart was set on studying racial differences, but at the time, I didn't want to be seen as "difficult." Although my advisor seemed open to my research idea, I feared that the rest of my dissertation committee would find my idea "too radical." No one else in the program was studying race and racism at that time, and I was more concerned with white comfort than I was with focusing on a topic that I really wanted to study. I ended up focusing my dissertation instead on invisible identities. I felt like that topic was much more palatable to everyone, especially my committee members. One of the ways that whiteness functions is convincing non-white people that we should not be talking about and bringing up race. Conversations about race, and more specifically racial differences, scare many white people and make them feel uncomfortable. Although my particular cohort was racially and ethnically diverse (out of eight of us, four were non-white), the topics we chose still had to be acceptable to our white professors and program administrators in order to be approved. I didn't want to "rock the boat." I stuck to a dissertation topic that felt "more acceptable" because I was centering whiteness by prioritizing the feelings of my classmates, professors, and dissertation committee who might have been put off by a dissertation study on race.

. . .

As you've seen, much of my life has been rooted in chasing invisible standards of whiteness. I hope that learning more about my experiences and how I centered whiteness throughout my life has sparked self-reflection about the ways you may have done so in your own life. In order to decenter whiteness within us, awareness is vital. You cannot change something you don't fully understand. A large part of what I hope you're gaining from this book is greater awareness about how whiteness is centered in your workplace and how we've all centered whiteness in our own lives. So, then, how can we start to decenter whiteness in our lives?

Consuming Content

One way that I've decentered whiteness is through the content I consume, whether it's an article I read, a book I listen to, or a video I watch on YouTube. Content has helped me understand and recognize the ways that whiteness has been centered in my own life. In my workshops, I usually provide workshop attendees with some creators to follow—writers, influencers, or activists that develop content that is educational. I encourage you to think about communities and groups outside of your own that you know very little about. Learning more about communities and groups that I don't know much about has taught me how whiteness has been centered in my own learning and education.

For a *Forbes* piece, I had a chance to interview Sevil Suleymani, an Azerbaijani Turk who grew up in Iran, about the women's revolution taking place in Iran following the September 2022 death of Mahsa Amini while she was in police custody. Suleymani talked about how the United States plays such an integral role in the public perception of Iran. Sitting down and chatting with her for that interview made me recognize how some of my perceptions of Iran have been based on what I heard and saw in the media, and more specifically white and Eurocentric media.

We saw this personified in the coverage from the Russo-Ukrainian War that escalated in February of 2022. The media seemed to be more sympathetic to Ukrainians than other communities in war-torn populations. One senior foreign news correspondent remarked that Ukraine "isn't a place … like Iraq or Afghanistan, that has seen conflict raging for decades. [Kyiv] is a relatively civilized, relatively European … city, where you wouldn't expect that." In a separate news segment, the former deputy prosecutor general of Ukraine remarked that the conflict was especially emotional for him because it was "European people with blue eyes and blond hair being killed."[4] The underlying implication was that war and conflict are only "supposed" to happen in "third-world countries."

NOTE I'm using the term *third-world* here for emphasis, but I *do* want to point out that the term itself is white-centered, as I mentioned in an earlier chapter. Third-world countries are specifically underresourced and underdeveloped because of a targeted effort by Western nations to extract resources and land through force from different Indigenous populations around the world.

Pause and think about the groups and communities you don't know a lot about.

Then think about mediums you can utilize to expand your awareness. Given all my struggles with weight fluctuations my entire life, I knew I needed to deprogram my mind when it comes to my thoughts about weight and health. I love following size discrimination activists that I can learn more from and who help me to decenter whiteness in the ways I think about weight and size. I also try to be intentional about following folks who are educators in sex and gender because my binary thinking and traditional upbringing influence the ways that I view gender identity. Be intentional about seeking out education to decolonize your white-centered views. Also, take stock of who you follow online. Curate your social media timeline so that you're consuming content from folks that are expanding your awareness and understanding about communities you don't know much about.

Cultivating Community

My community plays an integral role in keeping me accountable. I try to be intentional about surrounding myself with folks who will "check me," so to speak, when I say or do things that are out of pocket. I try to surround myself not with "yes people" who will just agree with everything I say and do, but with people who will challenge me and push me to do better and be better. Part of that includes the community I cultivate online. Many of the people I choose to follow have become my community members in some form or fashion, and I'm able to talk with them and learn from them and vice versa. They keep me accountable. I also believe those that follow me online keep me accountable for the things I write, say, and do, and I try to welcome and be open to feedback and critique. Find your community of people that will hold you accountable. Pause to assess whether the folks you're with the most are likely to critique you or push you to think in ways that will help you to grow. The friends I've made since high school and college are the ones that know me well, and they hold me accountable. So do the folks I've met along the way and throughout my career through different in-person and online communities that I've developed friendships with. I don't enjoy being around people who agree with every single thing I say. We all need to break out of our echo chambers and engage with folks who will hold us accountable in order to decenter whiteness within ourselves.

Practicing Humility

One trait I'm always trying to sharpen is humility. It makes me smile when I meet people and they tell me that they love how humble I am. I hope that sharing this doesn't make me seem like I lack humility, but it's something I strive for. As a person who has been able to accomplish many material things, I sometimes enter spaces where people are enamored with the things I do or have done. It's easy to let that sort of thing go to your head. In his book *Ego Is the Enemy*, Ryan Holiday discusses how vulnerable we start to become when we let compliments go to our heads. We start thinking we are infallible, and that's when our growth stagnates. The rejections and barriers that we experience actually keep us humble.

I love when I am corrected by someone because it reminds me that I am deeply flawed and imperfect. I always remind my clients that I am not an "expert" and that I am liable to make mistakes, just like them. Think about these questions: How do you keep yourself humble? What do you do to keep yourself "in check"? It may be the people you surround yourself with or the criticism you receive. Don't push those critiques aside. Listen to what people are saying and recognize that some of these critiques may be very valid. Being able to take criticism and recognize when it's coming from a place of truth is an invaluable skill that will help us on our quest to decenter whiteness. Staying in a place of humility will help us when we inevitably are corrected for operating in a place of white-centeredness. If I think I can do no wrong, when I *do* actually deserve or need criticism and critique, I may refuse it because I've pedestalized myself, preventing me from hearing and listening to the valid criticisms.

Lastly, when moving toward a framework of decentering whiteness, it's important to ask yourself: Do I want this particular thing in my life because I truly desire it or because whiteness has told me that I should want it? When I ask myself that question, I'm astonished at what comes up for me. Many of the material possessions I've desired throughout the years were rooted in my desire for whiteness. I equated these things—a PhD, a "good job," being thin, having straight hair—with the pinnacle of white perfection that I've always been striving for. I thought achieving those accolades and having those accomplishments would make me a "good Black person," shielding me from the racism and anti-blackness that in reality is inescapable. Understand that decentering whiteness within us will be a lifelong journey because we've spent our entire lives to this point centering whiteness, but we must never stop striving for it.

9
centering the most marginalized employees

Five months before I left academia, I started writing my resignation letter. At that point, my consultancy had grown and I had been partnering with many organizations and institutions that realized they needed an equity consultant. I often considered what life would be like if I left the university and focused all my energy on serving workplaces. When I wrote the first draft of my resignation letter, it was four pages long; I felt like Aaliyah when she sang her song "4 Page Letter." In the letter I explained, line by line, all the qualms I had with the university and more specifically my department and how it had handled issues in the past. I also mentioned how I felt the university and academia in general wasn't a safe space for Black women. Here is an excerpt:

> I've been teaching at [this university] for the last five years and I've been teaching in academia for over seven years. When I arrived at [this university], everyone was friendly and I thought this was an environment that would allow me to grow as an individual as

well as an academic. But after my tenure at this university, it is abundantly clear that any claims of [this university] prioritizing diversity, equity, inclusion and belonging are lip service. As someone who works in the diversity, equity, inclusion and belonging (DEIB) space and runs a consultancy where I help corporations navigate their DEIB issues, my repeated attempts to change the environment in this institution have failed and I no longer want to pour anymore time, energy or effort into trying to make this a better place.

I continued with a line-by-line explanation of some of the micro- and macroaggressions I had experienced in the five years that I worked at the institution. After I submitted my resignation email, my direct manager, who didn't respond even though they were directly mentioned multiple times in my letter, sent out an email to the department congratulating a fellow professor that had been featured in a golf article. I almost wanted to be shocked. No one I specifically called out for causing me harm while in the university ever offered me any words of apology or acknowledged their wrongdoing, even though I cc'd the university president along with every single person I named directly in my letter. I was later told that the university was trying to escape culpability (and likely a lawsuit) because I'd stated in my resignation letter that the university, as is true across academia, is often unkind to Black professors. Even though I specifically called out the institutional inequities, exclusion, and micro- and macroaggressions I experienced, there was zero remorse or repentance from the university or the offending parties.

The irony of my particular situation is that just weeks before I resigned, my manager had emailed me asking if I would help the university secure a DEI grant. A year prior, after seeing the increased interest in DEI, that same manager had assigned me the task of creating a DEI certificate program for the department. It was something I was assigned to do because my colleagues recognized that DEI was my domain and that I owned a DEI consultancy. Yet and still, when I made suggestions and offered advice about how to create a safer campus for people from underrepresented racial groups, no one listened to me or my advice. My university and my experiences are not unique. Many organizations and institutions push talent out in similar ways by not centering the feelings, experiences, and feedback of their most marginalized employees.

Why Is It Important to Center Marginalized Employees?

We cannot have a conversation about decentering whiteness in the workplace without acknowledging the necessity to center the most racially marginalized and oppressed populations. Why is it important to center these populations? Two poignant ways to think about this question are the curb-cut effect and the triage method.

The basic idea of the curb-cut effect is that when we create interventions, laws, and programs that are designed to benefit the most vulnerable populations (disabled people, racially marginalized communities, the elderly, etc.), everyone else ends up benefiting as well.[1] A great example of this is when it comes to accessibility. When I'm perusing social media, I'm often in a place that doesn't allow me to listen to videos with the volume up. A surprising number of videos on social media don't contain closed captioning. Although many social media platforms have auto-captions, they're not always accurate. Video content is difficult to watch when there are no captions or the auto-generated captions don't work properly. Even though closed captioning is a way to make your content more accessible to those who are Deaf or hard of hearing, adding closed captioning to your videos helps everyone out.

The curb-cut effect was originally spearheaded to create a more equitable and accessible world for people with disabilities. A curb cut is an opening on a curb that allows easy access to a road, sidewalk, or driveway. Initially designed for people in wheelchairs, the curb cut is helpful to everyone. For example, folks with strollers can move more easily into the street when there's a curb cut.[2] A good way to think about it is this: "When we ignore the challenges faced by the most vulnerable among us, those challenges, magnified many times over, become a drag on economic growth, prosperity, and national well-being."[3]

The triage method is a standard practice in healthcare where during emergency situations, those who have the most severe and life-threatening injuries receive care first. In a poignant article, Amira Barger explained how the triage method could also be applied to workplace DEI efforts.[4] Healthcare professionals are encouraged to ask different questions to ascertain the individual patient's condition. Temperature, blood pressure, and other vital signs are taken to determine the severity of an illness or injury. If we think about our workplace in the same way, we can design interventions with the most marginalized and harmed populations in mind.

We can think about DEI practitioners similar to how we think of doctors: each of us has a different specialty. I specialize in racial equity and justice, and I have experience diagnosing workplace issues and prescribing "medicine" in the form of specific interventions aimed at racial equity. In my experience, many organizations and institutions enlist the help of practitioners that have a different specialty than what they need. They find a gastroenterologist to help them with their heart issues when what they actually need is a cardiologist. If racism and a lack of racial equity is what your organization is facing, for example, it's imperative to find the right "doctor" to help you diagnose the issue and prescribe effective treatment.

In our workplaces, we should be designing programs, policies, and interventions with the most marginalized in mind. Doing this requires a deep understanding of who experiences the most harm and oppression within your workplace. Having this understanding will help you think about how to start prioritizing their needs. Use the triage method to determine which employees in your workplace are experiencing the most workplace harm and need attention first. To determine which employee "injuries" are the most severe, you have a few options.

Qualitative Analysis

As mentioned, for several of my clients, I've conducted a qualitative analysis to better understand the experiences of different employees. One of my former clients was a large healthcare provider. I conducted a qualitative analysis for the client by interviewing the healthcare professionals within a particular division of the organization. The focus of the analysis was to gain a deeper understanding of the unique issues that underrepresented racial groups were facing. Because I was an external consultant, the healthcare professionals I spoke with seemed to feel comfortable sharing their issues and their qualms on their specific team. I collected qualitative data by having one-on-one conversations with a group of employees that volunteered to share their experiences. I took detailed notes of our conversations and then reviewed them to search for themes that emerged. Based on these themes, I was able to identify specific issues and recommend targeted interventions to address them. This is one of the best ways to understand the needs of the most marginalized employees. Much of our focus when collecting DEI data is often on quantitative analyses. While numbers are important and give us relevant information, they don't tell the full story. Qualitative data gives us more information about the *whys* of workplace DEI issues.

Focus Groups

Focus groups—simply a collective of employees willing to provide feedback about their experiences—can be a great way to garner feedback from marginalized employees. I prefer one-on-one conversations so that no one's experience is biasing anyone else's, but focus groups are the next best thing if time is limited. Gather a group of employees, ideally those from a particular group, and gauge their comfort with sharing their workplace experiences. Sometimes employees won't feel comfortable sharing unless they know that what they say will be kept confidential. Engage with an equity consultant or utilize your HR department or internal DEI team to help facilitate the focus groups. Develop a set of questions that will help you understand their workplace experiences. Consider how you'll store the information shared. In my experiences, it's best that the information provided is kept confidential to make employees feel more comfortable sharing and being transparent.

Strategies to Center the Most Marginalized Employees

After conducting qualitative analyses, focus groups, and other data collection methods on the experiences of marginalized employees, you can introduce specific strategies to prioritize their needs in your workplace.

Specificity

One frequent comment I hear when working with clients is that by prioritizing marginalized employees, you are somehow excluding others. The opposite is actually true. By recognizing who requires the most support and then creating interventions to address these needs, *everyone* in your workplace will benefit.

Sometimes that benefit will be clear: a sponsorship program, for example, designed to help Black employees ascend can be beneficial if used by all employees. Although the goal behind the program's creation may be to improve advancement outcomes for your Black talent, it could end up benefiting other employees in the organization. In other instances, the ways that specific and tailored interventions benefit all employees may not be as clear-cut and tangible, but your workplace should still consistently create interventions to support underrepresented racial groups. Work is a better place when employees feel a sense of belonging. A study by Great Place to Work found that when employees experience belonging in the workplace, they are three times more likely to say their workplace is fun and three times more likely to feel that people look forward to coming to work.[5] At times, there will be interventions needed that will benefit only a segment of your employee population. Communicating about the existing disparities, how they impact different racialized populations, and why a particular program, initiative, or intervention is needed can help gain employee buy-in and may reduce resistance when you introduce targeted interventions. Understanding the needs of your different employee populations is vital.

Specificity is critical when it comes to centering the most marginalized employee populations. I often find that people have a strong desire to lump everyone together. BIPOC (Black, Indigenous, and People of Color), used as a catch-all phrase to describe any non-white person, has become one of my least favorite terms. My first issue with it is that it's not inclusive of all the myriad ethnicities and groups. It's specific in that Black and Indigenous populations are specifically called out and identified, which is important. But other populations (Pacific Islanders, South Asians, and Middle Easterners, for example) are all lumped in as "people of color." A South Asian employee once asked me if they were able to join their company's BIPOC affinity group. The employee explained that they didn't know if they identified as a "person of color," so they didn't know whether the BIPOC affinity group was inclusive of the South Asian population.

My second issue with the term BIPOC is that it erases the similar but very unique experiences that those within different racial and ethnic groups face. Although both Arabs and Black Americans, for example, may experience discrimination, their marginalization manifests in different ways and therefore their experiences are unique. If we want to center the *most* marginalized employees, we have to recognize that different groups of non-white employees have different experiences. I heard influencer and psychotherapist Dr. Raquel Martin once say that she is intentional about focusing her work as a therapist specifically on the Black community. She explained that doing so helps her in her work and allows her to better understand the needs of this community in order to provide more personalized care and support.

Tailored Interventions

It is vital that the interventions you develop are created with marginalized employees in mind. Through your data collection and analysis, you'll be able to figure out what programs your marginalized employees need. In a lot of the workplaces I enter, one of the most common issues I see is racially marginalized employees feeling like they're not being provided with the tools needed to advance in their workplace. Mentorship and sponsorship programs are particularly beneficial for non-white employees and especially non-white women. However, these specific interventions aren't always a reality. Those who are tapped to mentor and sponsor junior employees often don't have the time needed to dedicate to these endeavors. If mentorship and sponsorship from senior employees isn't feasible, you may have to seek outside help. Think about external coaching and how that could be integrated into your workplace. A connection of mine, Angelina Darrisaw, owns a coaching company, C-Suite Coach, specifically designed to source coaches and provide DEI programming to support minoritized employees by equipping them with the tools they need to advance and thrive in their workplace. You must first determine who has the greatest needs and then follow by figuring out how you will address these needs.

In 2020, after a friend asked me about the impact of my racial equity workshops, I started collecting data on them. I was able to share the data with this friend, who analyzed and used it to complete their doctoral dissertation. The dissertation was examining white racial identity and whether workplace diversity trainings, specifically those that focused on anti-racism and racial equity, influenced the white racial identity development of the white employees. According to Helms's White Racial Identity Model, there are six stages involved in racial identity development for white people, some of which are guilt, denial, an understanding of systemic racism, and the awareness of one's own whiteness. At the last stage of the identity model, whites develop an understanding of their own white racial identity as well as an awareness and acceptance of racial, ethnic, and cultural differences among communities.[6] When they reach this stage, Helms theorizes that white people will be committed to anti-racism. My friend was interested in assessing whether racial equity workshops were instrumental in influencing the development of white racial identity, thus impacting anti-racism efforts for white employees.

To collect the data, I gave employees a pre- and post-survey before and right after my racial equity workshop. The results indicated that although diversity training *did* increase "commitment to ethnic identity" in white employees, the results after one training session were small. The research may, however, provide an indication of the "positive" effects of a series of DEI trainings on white participants. For the dissertation, data from non-white employees was collected but not considered since the focus of the research was on white employees. As I mentioned before, much of the focus when we consider the efficacy of DEI training is on whether it will change the hearts and minds of white people. This is one of the ways we center whiteness in our DEI interventions. What's important to consider is the perceptions of marginalized employees after a workshop and other DEI interventions.

To truly center the most marginalized, we have to consider their feelings and perspective with every single intervention that we introduce. A few years ago, I was conducting a qualitative analysis and I got some interesting feedback from an employee. The employee, who was Middle Eastern, shared with me that he found it highly problematic that his organization had offered a workshop on identifying microaggressions but the person facilitating the workshop was white. He said that this in itself was a microaggression. Consider issues like this when you're deploying DEI training and workshops. Some DEI interventions get a bad rap (DEI training, for example). I don't think that's because these trainings completely suck, but in part because we're measuring the wrong thing. We have to decenter whiteness when measuring the effectiveness of our DEI interventions and ensure we are creating tailored interventions for our most marginalized employees.

Education

After you've obtained feedback from your most marginalized employees, it's important to use that feedback to design educational programs that address gaps. What are the issues that are perpetuated in your organization or institution? Provide programming, bring in speakers, and facilitate discussions and workshops to increase awareness and understanding. Some really important topics that I don't see enough in education programming include caste bias, colorism, hair discrimination, accent discrimination, and the impacts of generational trauma.

When thinking about education, it's also imperative to equip leaders with the tools to address systemic inequities. Far too often, I see the promotion of topics that don't address the root cause of bias. For example, we hear a lot of conversations about imposter syndrome, and much of the advice focuses on how to help marginalized groups move past it and how to empower those that have it. We don't talk about how imposter syndrome doesn't actually exist but is the result of an environment that has made those deemed as "other" feel like they're inadequate. How do we change the environment that caused people to feel imposter syndrome in the first place? We're not getting at the source of the inequity. Salary negotiation is another topic that is promoted but doesn't target the root cause of pay inequities. Research has shown that even when women *do* negotiate their salaries, they don't get the salaries they ask for. It's not that women aren't asking for higher pay—women ask for raises as often as men. Systemic barriers mean that when women *do* ask, they are penalized more for it.[7]

Similarly, the popular piece of career advice given to job seekers and job-incumbents must be more nuanced. Career advisors suggest self-promotion as a way to advance and move up within your organization. A recent study found that not all employees benefit from self-promotion, however. When compared with other racial groups, Black employees are actually penalized for self-promotion.[8] Rather than offering broad-brush advice, it's important to recognize and understand the root causes of many of our workplace inequities and provide a more nuanced approach that takes this into consideration. Leaders should be trained on how to address these issues rather than training employees on how to navigate systemic inequities.

Safer Spaces

Centering the most marginalized employees requires you to ensure that you're not just focusing on getting employees of different backgrounds into the workplace but that you're working equally hard to make sure that they feel valued and safe once there. When I start working with new clients, I often find that diversity is the sole goal. I understand why. Diversity, and particularly racial and ethnic diversity, is one of the only visible markers of DEI "progress." If an organization or institution doesn't have racial or ethnic diversity, it is considered a "failure." So much of the emphasis and focus within DEI has been solely on getting more "diverse" candidates in the door. But it's a bad idea to focus so heavily on getting underrepresented groups into the workplace without giving an equal amount of attention to ensuring that these individuals actually feel safe and are being invited into a welcoming environment.

In many of the jobs I've worked in, I've been "the only." In many cases I left because the environment wasn't welcoming to me. As I've mentioned, my decision to leave academia was because it has proven an unsafe place for me as a Black woman. Make sure that you're investing an equal amount of time, effort, and resources into ensuring that the environment not only is inclusive and fosters a sense of belonging but also is built around equitable policies, practices, processes, and procedures. Include employees, particularly those from marginalized communities, into the decision-making process. Marginalized employees shouldn't simply be an afterthought; prioritize them at every level in the workplace.

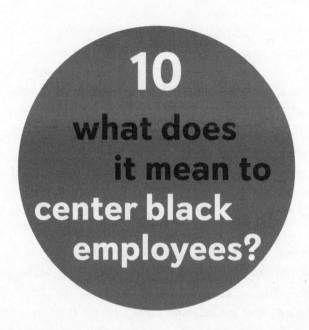

10

what does it mean to center black employees?

One of my favorite quotes comes from the Combahee River Collective, a group of Black feminists: "If Black women were free, it would mean that everyone else would have to be free since our freedom would necessitate the destruction of all the systems of oppression."[1] That quote illustrates what the primary focus of workplace DEI efforts should be: removing systemic barriers for the most harmed and vulnerable population. In her Pulitzer Prize–winning book *Caste*, Isabel Wilkerson examines racial hierarchies in the United States. She argues that similar to the caste system that exists within Indian society, the US has a racial caste system that puts Black Americans at the bottom of the hierarchy.[2] We cannot disregard the historic exclusion, subjugation, and harm that Black Americans have endured in the United States. Black people often experience the most severe forms of harm and marginalization outside of the US as well. As this chapter will discuss, anti-blackness is global.

It's impossible to have a conversation about how whiteness is centered in our workplaces without also examining how pervasive anti-blackness is. While it's imperative to discuss how decentering whiteness requires us to center racially marginalized employees, there are equally important reasons to focus specifically on our Black employee population. In the previous chapter we discussed how the triage method is used in healthcare to prioritize patients that have the most life-threatening injuries and illnesses. In many modern workplaces around the world, employees who identify as Black or who have darker complexions experience the most severe forms of subjugation and harm, so they must be triaged first. If there's anything you must take away from this chapter and this book, it's this: *the best way to decenter whiteness in your workplace is to prioritize, amplify, uplift, and center those that experience the most oppression and harm.*

On LinkedIn not too long ago, I saw a post that infuriated me. I don't remember who wrote it, but the post stated that you can't call yourself a DEI practitioner if you focus only on Black people. Even more frustrating was that the post was written by a Black person. The upside of the anger I feel sometimes when I'm scrolling through social media is that it often inspires my writing. That LinkedIn post was a catalyst for a *Forbes* article I wrote titled "Does DEI Focus Too Much on Black People?"[3] In that article I explained why the claim that the DEI field focuses "too much" on Black people is a wild assertion based on a lack of knowledge and awareness regarding how oppression manifests. The question itself is anti-black.

The Global History of Anti-blackness

It's important to briefly mention some history. Outside of the United States, different groups of Black or African peoples have experienced marginalization. I've discussed some of these groups in previous articles and also in my book *The Pink Elephant*, but it's worth reiterating here:[4]

INDIA India has a three-thousand-year-old caste system that impacts how people are treated in the present day. In this social stratification system, people are placed into different categories that signify their social standing. There are specific patterns found in caste groups; for example, people with lighter skin complexions tend to, on average, be in the upper castes.[5]

India also includes an ethnic group called the Siddis, who are descended from the Bantu people in East Africa and were brought to India and enslaved by the Arabs, Portuguese, and British. The Siddi people have darker skin tones and experience being ignored and erased from Indian society. Many work as farmers and manual laborers.

PALESTINE Amnesty International indicates that Palestinians experience routine systemic discrimination.[6] For Afro-Palestinians, the oppression and discrimination they face is much more severe.

AUSTRALIA Indigenous (formerly called Aboriginal) Australians have phenotypes that are closer to African, and they experience racism and discrimination in Australia. There are also indications that Indigenous Australians experience a combined form of oppression, racism, and ableism on a systemic level.[7]

LATIN AMERICA Within Latin America, colorism is rampant. A persistent issue that activists and public figures have pointed out is the lack of representation within Latin American media. Dominican-American singer and entertainer Amara La Negra has spoken extensively about the racism and colorism she experienced as a darker-skinned Afro-Latina.[8]

AFRICA As in Latin America, within different parts of Africa, skin-bleaching creams and other products designed to lighten (and whiten) one's skin remain popular. These products are highly dangerous and contain chemicals that are harmful to a person's health.[9]

There's a common misconception that anti-blackness is a pervasive issue only in the United States. I was having a conversation recently with someone from London, who was pointing out how racist America is to Black people. I found it ironic that someone from Britain was saying this, given Britain's long and extensive colonial history. Pervasive anti-blackness within the United States may be more widely known and understood because of the far reach of American media, but we can't neglect that anti-blackness is a global issue and didn't start in the United States. In every single society where Black people are not the majority, and even in societies where Black people *are* the majority (South Africa, for example), subjugation, marginalization, and oppression have ensued. It's important to be aware of this and not assume that it's just a US issue.[10]

Let's go back to that LinkedIn post asserting that DEI practitioners who focus only on anti-blackness are not equipped to call themselves DEI practitioners. Anyone who understands how pervasive anti-blackness is will know why this statement is so problematic. If you recognize how Black people have been treated within different societies throughout history, you should understand why it's so necessary to focus on Black people specifically within our DEI work, as Isabel Wilkerson states so poignantly in *Caste*. Her book focuses mostly on the racial hierarchy within the United States, and she elucidates why it's important that our interventions be designed with the most marginalized populations in mind. If we adopt the triage method that Amira Barger suggests, then we should always be thinking of the most minoritized and historically excluded populations when addressing DEI needs. To revisit the words of the Combahee River Collective, we will be liberated only when the most marginalized communities are free.

My Experiences with Anti-blackness

When reflecting on my own life, I've faced anti-blackness in different ways, many of them in my school experiences. I shared in chapter 8 that when I was younger my family lived in Oman, where I attended a British school and experienced pervasive anti-blackness because of my physical features. As I mentioned, my classmates would constantly make fun of my lips and the size of my lips. The wild part is that it was the non-white kids who were making fun of me the most! Children learn quickly to adopt anti-black behaviors in our society. Being outside of the US in a Middle Eastern country didn't magically shield me from anti-blackness.

When we returned to the US, I attended a private school in rural Minnesota. My white male classmates made remarks about my body, and my butt specifically. Though I was on the thinner side, by white standards I was a bit chubby. Looking back now, I'm able to catch how racialized these remarks were. I remember one of my white classmates saying I had a "ghetto booty" and I somehow thought it was a compliment because I had a crush on him. At this same private school, I was constantly getting in trouble because of my outfits. Although the skirts I wore were the same length as those of my white counterparts, I was always sent to the office for violating the school's dress code. My mom recounts being called numerous times. Although I didn't realize it at the time, I was targeted for being one of the only Black kids out of hundreds of students; I was hyper-scrutinized.

Outside of school, I felt like I was treated differently from my peers, particularly in the workplace. The pervasive scrutiny I received while in academia provided me with concrete evidence of differential treatment. In one university I worked in, I received an excessive amount of criticism compared to my peers. My students frequently called me by my first name, even though I observed that they didn't do this with any of their other professors, and I emphasized that they should call me Dr. Janice. In many instances I had the same or more academic credentials than my peers, and yet the othering continued.

When I worked in academia, my email signature listed my title as Assistant Professor in the Management Department. One afternoon, I received an email from the department chair explaining that she had received a complaint about an "incorrect title" in my email signature and I needed to change it. The complainant wanted me to put "clinical" in front of the assistant professor title to denote my non-tenure-track status. Apparently, it was important to let all the other faculty members and students know that although I had a PhD like my peers, I was not on the same level as them. It was such a preposterous ask, and even the department chair admitted that she thought the request was unorthodox.

The hyper-scrutiny and hyper-surveillance I experienced is common for Black employees.[11]

In chapter 3, I shared the experience where my course was taken away from me because a group of students complained about me. Despite the fact that my syllabi were created by the program director (a white man) and I structured my course so that he and I were teaching the students in an almost identical way, the students felt they weren't learning in my class. They were "too scared" to talk to me about their concerns, so they decided to complain to my boss and his boss instead. My experiences with anti-blackness in academia were often quite subtle, but a few were overt, conspicuous macroaggressions.

The problem with anti-blackness and the reason why it's so difficult to eradicate is that all of us can fall victim to it—even Black people. As a collective, we are able to recognize and point out the harms that white supremacy culture causes, but we have a more difficult time recognizing how we've *all* swallowed and digested the anti-blackness that was fed to us at birth. We often have an easier time pointing out white supremacists than we do recognizing and admitting that we are being used as pawns (whether willingly or unwillingly) in a system that prioritizes whiteness.

Centering Black Employees

Blackness and whiteness exist as opposites. Because whiteness is centered, blackness is penalized and vilified. Now, we could have a whole other discussion on how Black proximity to non-Black people has become profitable, popular, and trendy. But I'll save that for another book (although I have touched on blackfishing in chapter 6 and in *The Pink Elephant*). For Black employees and employees that have some sort of proximity to blackness—whether through their identity, physical appearance and phenotype, name, speech and language, or other aspects of their individual identity—systemic racism can impact their experiences. Workplace policies, practices, processes, and procedures are designed with the white employee in mind. Deviating from the model of whiteness will result in harsh consequences, whether that's being less likely to be hired into a workplace or being rated less favorably on a performance evaluation. We don't consider Black employees when we're creating workplace systems, and that's a large part of the problem. The modern workplace is not designed with the most marginalized in mind. As you move toward decentering whiteness in your workplace, what are the ways that you can start centering Black employees?

Understanding That Representation Isn't Enough

The death of Tyre Nichols shook the world. Nichols was a twenty-nine-year-old unarmed Black man who was brutally beaten by several Memphis police officers in January of 2023. A few days after being hospitalized, Nichols passed away. Five of the police officers involved in Nichols's beating were Black.[12] The case sparked an important conversation about the pervasive nature of anti-blackness, even amongst Black people. Those officers couldn't see the humanity in someone that looked just like them. For me, and many of us within the Black community, Nichols's death was just a painful reminder of how indoctrinated we all are into anti-black systems and white-dominant culture. Anti-blackness is deadly.

In the Black community we have a popular saying, coined by author Zora Neale Hurston: "All skinfolk ain't kinfolk." The saying basically means that not everyone *in* your community is *for* your community. Being Black doesn't necessarily mean you are invested in the liberation of Black people. The way that whiteness and white supremacy culture works is that it's so effective at pitting different groups against each other that we often end up fighting under the false belief that we are enemies. Harvard University has hired the institution's first ever non-white president. I was elated when I heard this news, but I've been fooled into cheering about a new appointment before learning the individual's stance and personal politic.

We always hear that "representation matters," but we can't be focused on getting Black people in the door without first fixing the systemic issues that prevent them from feeling safe enough to stay. While representation is important, making sure that the folks being brought in are actually invested in centering Black people is imperative. It's not enough to hire and promote Black employees; you must also give them the tools, the team, the time, and the investments they need to thrive in their roles. It's also important to think about ways to vet the people that are brought into your organization, especially those who are put into leadership roles; assess them on metrics of equity to ensure they're invested in centering Black employees. You can gauge this by asking your Black employees for their opinions about prospective talent and by including questions in the employment interview to evaluate a candidate's desire to center Black employees specifically.

Centering Black Voices and Feedback

Your workplace equity efforts should always include input and feedback from Black people, especially because Black employees experience some of the most severe forms of subjugation, exclusion, discrimination, and harm in the workplace. Recently I saw a LinkedIn post by Adriele Parker expressing her frustration at a 2023 McKinsey report on DEI impact[13] that didn't include any Black authors.[14] Curious about the authors' backgrounds, I searched through their LinkedIn pages. Although the authors seemed to come from a few different racial/ethnic backgrounds, it was true that none of them were Black. I should note that at the end of the report, they included a blurb about how they'd sought out contributions from a number of different individuals, some of whom *were* Black. But it was troubling to see that such a detailed and thorough DEI report from a leading consultancy had somehow overlooked the voices and feedback of Black authors.

How often are you parsing out the feedback from your employees and seeing how Black employees specifically are feeling? As I've mentioned in previous chapters, disaggregating the data you receive is imperative; make sure you're not lumping all non-white employees into the same group. Specificity is vital. Are you looking for specific trends among employees? Be sure to familiarize yourself with the wealth of research that already exists about the Black employee experience. A simple yet effective question to ask Black employees is: What specific tools and resources do you need to thrive in your role? Set up focus groups specifically for Black employees.

An interesting example of when my voice as a Black DEI consultant was *not* centered happened in early 2022, when I was writing for a small publication that had reached out to me about paid writing opportunities. I was approached about writing a Black History Month piece and pitched several of my ideas to the editor that I'd been working with. For context, the editor was a white woman. After I wrote the piece and it was posted to their website, I noticed another Black History Month article, so I decided to check it out. When you open articles on the company's website, the first thing that pops up underneath the title is the author's name and photo. Before I even started reading the article, I noticed that a familiar face had written it. The author, whose name I won't share, was a South Asian woman whose posts frequently popped up on my LinkedIn feed. I was vaguely familiar with her, so I was confused when I saw that she had written a Black History Month article on what support looks like for Black employees. What infuriated me was that there were no Black voices included in her piece and she seemed to be speaking from the Black perspective. Her writing the piece was problematic for a number of reasons—namely, she was taking an opportunity away from a Black writer who should have written the piece, she was getting paid to write it, and she'd included no perspectives from Black people. I thought I was trippin'. I did more research on this person and found out that she was, in fact, not Black and didn't identify as Black but often referred to herself as "brown" on LinkedIn.

I reached out to the editor to ask her how that article got greenlit. I didn't expect a response since it was the weekend but received one within a few hours. The editor apologized profusely, thanked me for pointing this out, and promised the piece would be taken down. She also requested a meeting with me to talk through things further. I remember feeling happy that the company acquiesced to my concerns. When we had the requested meeting, the editor was joined by her colleague, a Black woman. I explained to both of them how problematic it was for a non-Black person to get paid to write about a Black experience she has never lived and asked how that piece could have gotten approved. I even gave them suggestions for vetting article pitches in the future to avoid this issue. What happened next was infuriating. The editor's Black colleague tried to explain to me that the writer was a "global DEI expert" and had worked in some large and well-known companies, so she was equipped to speak on the Black experience. I was flabbergasted to hear this coming out of a Black woman's mouth. How did she not understand how problematic this whole situation was?

After that meeting, there were a few back-and-forth emails, with them taking the article down, reposting it, and then taking it down again. What was most disconcerting was how someone who was a "global DEI expert" had thought it was acceptable to write this piece and, on top of that, get paid for it. It's unclear whether the writer knew what was happening behind the scenes, or whether she was even alerted to my complaint. That situation was a reminder of how engrained anti-blackness is, even amongst those of us who are considered "experts" in the space.

Make sure at every step in your workplace, you are centering Black voices—amongst your employees, your independent contractors, and even your customers. Get feedback about the Black customer experience. Sometimes when we hear stories of companies behaving badly, these are incidents where customers have been racially profiled. The 2018 Philadelphia Starbucks incident that ended up resulting in the arrest of two Black men was a perfect example. If you're collecting feedback from customers, are you parsing out that data to look for racial trends? What training and education are you providing employees with so that they recognize their own biases and they're not engaging in racist and anti-black behaviors toward customers? Racial profiling is still a big issue that Black customers face and can impact an organization's bottom line. No one wants to support a company that is racist and profiles its customers. The advent of social media makes it much easier now for companies to go viral for their racism. Think about what sort of education and training you can provide employees with so they're operating in an equity-driven and informed way.

Being Proactive, Not Reactive

To piggyback off that point, make sure you're implementing proactive versus reactive methods to equip employees with the tools and resources they need to be equitable and inclusive in their actions and behaviors. Organizations and institutions love to add unconscious bias trainings to their repertoire when called out for racism or discrimination. It's always better to have measures in place to prevent common issues rather than waiting until they actually occur. What measures do you have in place to make sure employees are continuously educated, that they recognize gaps in their awareness and understanding, and that they're being held accountable for their behavior and actions? I'm a big believer in having equity metrics that are assessed at every level within an organization or institution. Every person in a workplace has the ability to impact others, so DEI metrics must be developed and assessed at the start of employment and when job candidates are being evaluated, but also throughout an employee's tenure. I love to recommend that people complete the free Implicit Association Tests (IAT) from Harvard for their own knowledge and awareness (implicit.harvard.edu). There are a few that look specifically at our potential anti-black bias; consider asking every employee to take one. Are a number of employees showing a particular bias that is manifesting in the workplace? If so, think about developing programming that addresses these gaps and biases, rather than waiting until bigger issues arise and more harm is caused to fellow employees or a customer.

Providing Education

I can't state this enough: education is the key to centering Black employees. To center Black employees, you first must be aware of their needs. Some specific educational gaps I often see in my work include the following:

- Race-based hair discrimination is a widespread issue that many employees do not think about or understand. Consider bringing an educator in to explore the CROWN Act, which is legislation designed to provide protections against race-based hair discrimination.

- What is code-switching, why do Black employees do it, and how does it impact Black employees? As chapter 6 noted, code-switching is a linguistic phenomenon that occurs when a member of an underrepresented group changes the way they speak to fit the dominant culture.[15] People do this for many reasons, but if your employees are code-switching, getting to the root reason will help you decenter whiteness. Bring in an educator to explore this topic more.

- How does generational trauma affect your Black employees? Employees who are descendants of enslaved people experience generational trauma in a number of ways that are often overlooked. Black employees who come from war-torn countries may also experience generational trauma. How does this type of trauma impact Black employees specifically? Look into education that dives into this in more detail.

- How does our language promote anti-blackness? Racial dog whistles are important to be aware of. Some of the dialogue spewed by the anti-diversity segment of the population promotes harmful rhetoric that I have often seen repeated. When looking at specific social programs that were designed to benefit marginalized communities, it's important that we're having discussions that are fact-based. In the United States, for example, there's a commonly held belief that social programs like affirmative action and food assistance programs unfairly benefit Black people. This isn't accurate. Both affirmative action programs[16] and food assistance programs[17] have benefited the white community more than any other racial group.

- Colorism—the way that our systems and structures prioritize and prefer lighter-skinned individuals no matter their racial or ethnic group—is a pervasive issue in the workplace and beyond. For example, lighter-skinned Black people get shorter sentences on average than their darker-skinned counterparts.[18] It's important to educate *all* employees not only about systemic racism and anti-blackness but also about how colorism impacts employee experiences. Bring educators into your workplace who focus on this subject specifically. Two educators I would highly recommend are Dr. Sarah Webb and Tijidankay T.K. Sacco, who both have informative social media pages where they educate their audience on the pervasiveness of colorism.

- As mentioned in chapter 3, the Black tax is the result of the historic exclusion, systemic racism, and inequities that Black people in the United States experience. Lynette Khalfani-Cox explained it in a 2021 *Vox* article: "The reality is that for those of us able to generate wealth and reach a level of comfort, we are often also financially supporting family members or paying down debt. We simply don't have that generational wealth that so many white families have to fall back on and start out their adult lives with."[19] The result of all of these societal factors can take a toll on a Black person's experiences. Bring in educators and practitioners who can outline how historical exclusion and systemic racism have impacted different structures within society. Equity doesn't simply mean giving every employee enough resources; to truly center Black employees, you must have a deep understanding of their specific needs and what tools and resources you can provide to address these needs while also striving to rectify past harms.

- Understand the stigmas we all hold about blackness. This can show up in a number of ways, from the businesses we feel compelled to support to our desire to scrutinize Black people more.[20] My friend and I host a monthly LinkedIn Live show called *J/K . . . No but for Real*, where we chat about a number of topics, including our experiences engaging in anti-oppression work. One thing we've noticed is the difference in the number of people that attend our live show when we have the word *Black* in our episode title versus *white*: we have double the viewers for episodes with *white* in the name. It's important to note that our show's audience is mostly Black. This wasn't a surprising or shocking revelation for either of us, but it deserves mention. The stigmas we associate with blackness run deep.

- The erasure of Black voices and contributions is something that deserves consistent examination. I've written about this in the past, specifically when it comes to how Black women's contributions throughout history have been erased.[21] A few years ago, I fell victim to it myself. A Latine woman I'm connected with on social media reached out to me about hosting a Clubhouse conversation (Clubhouse is an audio platform that rose in popularity in late 2020). She wanted us to discuss how Black women and Latinas can come together to overcome our differences and combat anti-blackness. For context, the woman I would be facilitating the conversation with was a white-presenting Latina. I agreed and we planned to host the discussion and share it with our audiences. It wasn't until a friend of mine, Raven Rodriguez, pointed it out to me that I realized how problematic the discussion was. Raven explained that we were actively erasing individuals who identified as Afro-Latina through our title. We'd made the assumption that a person couldn't be *both* Black and Latina. Raven also pointed out that if we wanted to have a conversation about anti-blackness within the Latin American community, it was best to speak with someone who has *lived* experiences with that. Although I am Black, I am a lighter-skinned Black woman and I also don't identify as Latine. I can't speak specifically to anti-blackness within the

Latin American community. Likewise, because the woman I was hosting the panel with was a white Latina, she wasn't equipped to lead a conversation about anti-blackness since she had no lived experience with it. A white voice should *never* be centered in a conversation about anti-blackness. It took Raven pointing this out to me for me to realize how silly it would be for us to host that discussion. I hadn't considered how we were actively erasing the voices of Afro-Latine folks and how the structure of our discussion was inherently anti-black. When I reached out to the woman I'd be co-facilitating with to share this feedback, she pushed back and got defensive, saying something along the lines of people being haters and that this was even more of a reason to continue the conversation. Even when our active erasure of Black voices is pointed out, we so badly want to revert to white-centering ways. (We didn't go through with that discussion and I ended up changing the topic to focus on women's empowerment.)

In regards to education, after employees have an understanding of systemic racism, it's important to think about microreparations and what they could look like in your workplace for your Black employees. A history of redlining, subprime mortgage loans, racism in healthcare systems, and even pervasive issues like Black maternal mortality can be addressed through microreparations. In your workplace, microreparations could be specific programs to support the growth and advancement of your Black employees. What tools, for example, can you provide your Black employees who are expectant parents? You could bring in a Black birthing expert to provide the expectant parents with additional support and information to support Black maternal mortality rates. Are your Black employees more impacted by student loan debt? What resources can you provide to your Black employees who are affected by this and other types of debt? You could bring in experts to provide support around this particular issue. There are so many possibilities. In a recent article I wrote something that seemed to really resonate with many people, so I'll repeat it here: "We cannot be afraid to reimagine a new tomorrow simply because we don't have all the answers today."[22]

Understanding the ways that systemic racism has persisted should be an important part of your education and microreparations programs. Black employees, for example, sleep less on average than their non-Black counterparts.[23] What resources can you provide Black employees with so that they can have better and deeper sleep? One *Harvard Business Review* article suggested allowing Black employees to "call in Black" when racial mega-threats occur against the Black community.[24] Think about what systemic issues within your workplace may be exacerbating these issues. It's important to understand that in some cases, microreparations in your workplace may not address the systemic societal issues, but they can "stop the bleeding" in a sense and mitigate future harm. Train managers specifically on anti-blackness—what it is and how it manifests. Make this training ongoing. Also consistently measure the levels of equity that Black employees perceive in your workplace. You must be able to acknowledge the harms that have been caused to Black people globally. Microreparations offer an opportunity to consider ways to repair these injustices in small but tangible ways in your workplace.

Stopping the Performance

We cannot forget those promises and pledges that were made post–George Floyd. How are you backing up your words, and where are your DEI receipts? It's not enough to make public proclamations; your actions must align with your words. Ask Black employees how they feel you've done as a workplace in the wake of Floyd's murder. Ask for suggestions on how to support your Black employees. A few years ago, a large organization announced it was donating millions of dollars to support Black women business owners. I thought it was interesting that such an exorbitant amount was being put toward this endeavor when little had been said about how the corporation was supporting its Black women employees. If you have an open position in your workplace and you're interviewing candidates, imagine that a job-seeker asks you this question: What are you doing to support your Black employees? Donations to Black Lives Matter don't count. What specific actions are you engaging in now or could you engage in to elevate your Black employees? Think about this question long and hard and consider some of the actions mentioned in this chapter.

Embracing More Nuance

Centering Black employees requires more specificity and nuance. We must understand that although we should be introducing interventions that address the needs of our Black employees, they are not a monolith. It is problematic to lump all Black employees together. Recognize that—although they may all identify as Black—Caribbeans, Africans, and Black Americans have different experiences. Your Black immigrant employees may have different needs than your Black American employees. Race, ethnicity, and nationality all color our experiences. We must acknowledge this more in our work. A few years ago, I was asked to speak at an organization's Juneteenth event. The company is quite well known and part of me wanted to say yes, but being that I'm not a descendent of enslaved Africans in the United States, it felt icky to agree to take money and speak about a history that neither I nor my family members had personally experienced. Similarly, Black men, Black women, and Black nonbinary and trans folks have different experiences as well. We must keep this in mind. Though Black men, for example, may experience many of the same harms that Black women face, Black women face the dual layer of misogynoir: marginalization for their race *and* gender. Many of the harms that Black men face aren't identical to the experiences of Black women, so we must be cognizant of this distinction when creating support systems for Black employees in the workplace. Decentering whiteness in the workplace requires us to be as specific and nuanced as possible when we devise and design interventions to address the unique needs of the Black community.

11

steps to start decentering whiteness in the workplace

Now that you have all the tools to understand how whiteness is centered in the workplace, what is the first step to decentering it? Before we review that process, let's revisit the definition of white-centering offered at the beginning of this book: *actions and behaviors that prioritize, uplift, amplify, and venerate white people and white culture **above** other cultures and communities.*

There are three main components to decentering whiteness in the workplace. I love alliteration, so I developed a model called the 3 A's of Decentering Whiteness in the Workplace to make it easy to remember. The phases are illustrated in figure 11-1.

Step 1: Awareness

The first step to decentering whiteness in the workplace is recognizing that the issue exists. Some of the clients I work with are stuck in this particular phase. As mentioned in the beginning of this book, many

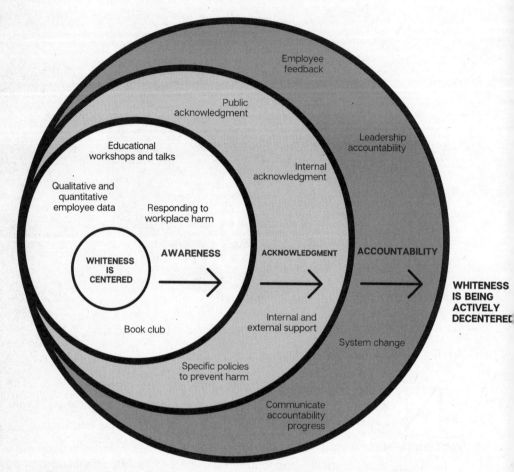

Figure 11-1: The Three A's of Decentering Whiteness in the Workplace

DEI interventions are unsuccessful because companies don't recognize how deeply whiteness is centered and how it's negatively impacting the workplace. You can raise awareness of the issue in a number of ways.

Qualitative and Quantitative Research

Data collection is a vital part of decentering whiteness. How are you assessing employee feedback? As we've explored in previous chapters, there are an infinite number of ways to collect employee feedback. Surveys are typically the most popular. I find that most businesses love to see quantitative data; they trust the numbers. I'm a bit biased about data collection: when it comes to employee sentiments about their particular workplace experiences, I'll always be in favor of qualitative data, which, although not numerical, gives you rich feedback that can be used to improve the workplace. Quantitative data doesn't really tell you the whole story. It gives you the what, but not the why. The why is always what we are seeking. Outside of surveys, you can assess qualitative data through focus groups, resignation letters, exit interview data, and customer feedback. Customers can provide a snapshot of how whiteness is centered based on their treatment by employees. Both qualitative and quantitative data can help you gain awareness of the issue.

Educational Workshops and Talks

I'm a big fan of educational workshops, panels, speaker series, and talks, and not simply because these are some of the interventions I do in addition to consulting. I'm in favor of any sort of employee and leadership education and development, but many overlook the value of this intervention. While I was in banking and in academia, we rarely had DEI-related talks or workshops, despite how much I wanted to see these types of learning opportunities.

An exorbitant amount of research claims that DEI trainings and workshops aren't effective. The general consensus is that these types of trainings are a waste of time and money. As we discussed in the previous chapters, the reason why this perception is so pervasive is because we're using a white measuring stick to evaluate these and other DEI interventions. When I come into an organization or institution, I'm asked to discuss a wide range of equity-related topics, including anti-blackness, hair discrimination, supporting marginalized communities, anti-racist hiring and retention practices, and similar subjects. When I finish a workshop or a speaking engagement, I often receive emails and direct messages from attendees from racially marginalized communities who enjoyed my facilitation. It warms my heart to hear how my presence, and the presence of these types of discussions, makes employees feel seen and a bit safer.

Education is a great preemptive tool for decentering whiteness in your workplace. You don't have to wait until a problem exists to address it. There will always be gaps in our awareness and understanding when it comes to communities outside of our own. What communities do you want to amplify and learn more about? Think about what the best ways to invest in employee education and development would be. All employees should have access to education and learning opportunities. Think about how you currently measure the effectiveness of education (if you measure it at all) and how you can expand the way you assess the return on investment of this type of intervention.

Workplace Incidents

Unfortunately, often it's not until a specific incident occurs that awareness is activated. Don't wait until your workplace goes viral to assess the environment that's been cultivated in your workplace. Have conversations with the HR department, which in many workplaces is the first line of defense when employees have issues and incidents. Is there a particular issue that keeps coming up with an employee, a group of employees, or on a particular team? Workplace incidents provide insights into the specific issues that your workplace is facing and ways in which whiteness is being centered.

Book Clubs

I know there have been some protests against employee book clubs. A few weeks after the murder of George Floyd in 2020, Tre Johnson wrote a great piece in the *Washington Post* called "When Black People Are in Pain, White People Just Join Book Clubs." The premise of the article was that book clubs aren't enough to upend the hundreds of years of mistreatment that Black people in the US have endured. When reflecting on white people, Johnson wrote

> what they do is never enough. This isn't the time to circle up with other white people and discuss black pain in the abstract; it's the time to acknowledge and examine the pain they've personally caused ... white people tend to take a slow route to meaningful activism, locked in familiar patterns, seemingly uninterested in really advancing progress. Theirs is still a world of signs and signaling, where actions like joining book clubs ... take precedence.[1]

I thought a lot about that piece when I stumbled upon it a few years ago. At the time, I'd been asked to lead my university's anti-racist book club but was overwhelmed and exhausted by the idea of having to guide my fellow colleagues on how to see my humanity as one of the only Black faculty.

I will say I am a bit biased. I grew up loving books. Reading was celebrated and encouraged in my household. *James and the Giant Peach* was the first chapter book I ever read. I recognize the transformative power of books and authors whose words can invoke emotions and catalyze thoughts that hadn't germinated prior to our reading them. I love the transferal of ideas as you're discussing a book with others. I miss being young and being assigned to read a book or having the teacher read out loud, followed by a group discussion of its meaning and implications. *The Gilded Cat* and *Tuck Everlasting* are forever etched into my memory, not necessarily because of the books themselves but because of the discussions we had with our teacher while reading.

Still, the book club critiques are valid. It's a compelling question to ponder: Outside of reading books and discussing them, what are we doing to put the information in them to use? I do think books can spark something in us that we hadn't previously realized, so I don't want to overlook their power, but I also don't want to promote overreliance on them. We can't fall into the trap of thinking that the books—or rather, our reading of them—equates to "doing the work." Books are simply a tool you can use on your journey, but they're useless if you're not applying what you read to everyday life.

Think about having a book club as a resource available to interested employees, but be mindful of the white-centering that is likely to result. As I mentioned, I was asked (several times) to lead the anti-racist book club in my university. I didn't personally ask to lead it, but ended up begrudgingly agreeing to do so. It ended up turning into a discussion with my white coworkers about racism. It was exhausting. Don't ask your non-white colleagues to lead your book club unless they specifically request to. Consider having someone outside your organization lead a book club discussion with employees. Bring me in to lead a book discussion on *Decentering Whiteness in the Workplace*. Also remember that life gets busy, and people don't always have time to read books. I'm a huge fan of audiobooks. Think about gifting interested employees with a yearlong subscription to access audiobooks as an additional resource to help increase awareness, to support learning and development, and to fill in gaps in their knowledge and understanding.

Step 2: Acknowledgment and Acceptance

Centering whiteness is an addiction that's hard to break free from. Because we're birthed into a world that centers whiteness, it can be challenging to divest from it, as my friend Joquina Reed would say. If we think of white-centering as an addiction that we're trying to overcome, it's helpful to look at the steps that those recovering from other addictions utilize. The first step in the popular twelve-step program is admitting that the problem exists. As an organization or institution, you must admit that whiteness is being centered in your workplace. This second step can be thought of as acknowledgment and acceptance. After you become aware of the problem (trust and believe, it's an issue in virtually every workplace), you must acknowledge and accept that it exists. This book should help you gain a deeper understanding of the ways that whiteness is centered in your workplace. How did you come to recognize that white-centering was a problem and in what ways does it exist? Maybe an incident happened or you conducted a qualitative analysis that made you aware of the issue. In what ways will you acknowledge that the problem exists?

Public Acknowledgment

Even if your workplace hasn't been the subject of public ridicule or outcry, it's important to publicly acknowledge your awareness of how you've engaged in problematic behavior in the past as an organization or institution. In 2008, the American Medical Association issued an apology specifically to Black physicians due to a century of "past wrongs."[2] In 2021, the American Psychological Association (APA) issued a statement to publicly apologize to people of color for "promoting, perpetuating, and failing to challenge racism, racial discrimination and human hierarchy in the U.S."[3] The Racial Revolution that followed the murder of George Floyd made many organizations and institutions reevaluate their systems and structures and think more about how they've perpetuated harm in the past.

In early 2022, the editorial board of the *Baltimore Sun*, Maryland's largest newspaper, issued an apology as well, stating that for decades the publication "promoted policies that oppressed Black Marylanders."[4] And in January of 2023, the American Society of Human Genetics (ASHG) apologized for its participation in the eugenics movement. The ASHG supported a number of harmful policies, including forced sterilization, and supported the use of genetics to validate discrimination against the Black community.[5] As these institutions have done, after you have awareness regarding how whiteness has been centered in your workplace, it's necessary to publicly acknowledge the harm you've caused in order to start making amends and repairing that harm.

Internal Acknowledgment

Think about whether an internal acknowledgment of harm is also necessary. Some of the clients I've worked with have issued a public apology or acknowledgment via internal channels. I think this is always a great idea, especially once you have enough information to recognize how harm has been committed in your workplace. Maybe you just did an equity audit and it revealed that some employees aren't advancing at the same rates as their counterparts. In addition to adjusting your advancement practices to rectify these inequities, you should acknowledge the wrongdoing. This is where I've seen many leaders struggle, similar to the difficulties we face when it comes to admitting our personal errors and wrongdoings. While there's often a mad rush to bury the mistakes or forget that they ever occurred, it's really powerful to be able to acknowledge where you've messed up or caused harm. No workplace is perfect or will ever be perfect. It's important to always have your ear to the streets as far as your workplace environment and culture so you're able to recognize how employees have been impacted and what their experiences are.

Internal and External Support

How will you continue to decenter whiteness in your workplace? What support is required to do this? Think about whether an internal or external DEI consultant would be beneficial to help you assess your workplace environment and understand the ways that whiteness is being centered. You could always bring me in to conduct a qualitative analysis or an equity audit for you. You may already have both internal DEI champions, like a chief diversity officer and a DEI team, and an external consultant that you work with. Think about whether there are additional supports needed to address decentering whiteness. Sometimes I'm brought in by organizations that already have a DEI team and a chief diversity officer, but they want me to speak on a particular issue that their DEI support team isn't equipped to answer, or they just want an additional resource. Think about what additional supports you need and how introducing them can serve as a powerful way to acknowledge your shortcomings as a workplace.

Workplace Harm

Having an awareness of the ways that your workplace centers whiteness will provide you with the tools you need to implement policies and practices that prevent harm. Allow this book to be your guide. Did you find out that your workplace has racist hiring practices? Did an employee reveal that your advancement and promotion processes are inequitable? The first part is diagnosing the issue. Once you know what the issue is, you have this book as a tool to keep coming back to as you start to strategize about the medicine and treatments your workplace needs to start healing. It's not enough to have the awareness that you center whiteness in your workplace, or even to admit that whiteness is embedded into your systems and structures. You must take consistent and concerted actions to decenter whiteness.

Some specific policies to prevent workplace harm include: 1) having an equity expert review your workplace procedures, practices, and processes on a consistent basis (annually or semiannually); 2) ensuring that there are anonymous feedback channels in your workplace and that the feedback shared is addressed; 3) having multiple people involved in workplace decision-making to lessen the likelihood of bias; and 4) ensuring that there's objective criteria utilized for practices like hiring and advancement.

Some of these same strategies can be used to respond to harm when it is inevitably committed. Having an anonymous feedback channel will let you know about smaller, seemingly more minor issues before they magnify into bigger problems. Not only can it be a preventative measure against harm, but an anonymous feedback channel can also help you to understand how to address the harm that has been caused. Make sure there's a clear structure in place and that leaders are trained on addressing and responding to harm. Are employees supposed to go directly to their manager, or is your HR department expected to deal with these types of issues? In my experiences teaching graduate students studying for the field of HR management, many students aren't adequately trained on skills like conflict resolution, crisis management, and navigating interracial conflict.

Have a system for dealing with issues related to workplace harm and be open to refining this system based on feedback. Make sure that employees understand what resources are available to them and that leaders are consistently trained and equipped with the tools to navigate, address, and mitigate workplace harm.

Old habits die hard. We'll always be ready to revert to our natural white-centric ways. It's an inevitable struggle that we'll endure throughout our lives. We must introduce policies that make it more difficult for us to center whiteness in our workplace.

Step 3: Accountability

The hardest part of decentering whiteness is holding people accountable. Out of the three steps, accountability is the one that workplaces struggle with the most. Accountability on any level can be difficult. It's easy to create interventions, introducing workshops on microaggressions and anti-racist hiring. It's easy to hire non-white employees. It's easy to make public statements and declarations. It's much, much harder to hold everyone accountable to the goals that are set forth to create a better and more equitable workplace. I understand why accountability is such a challenge. When I get to the accountability part of my leadership workshops and training, I see bodies shift—arms cross and faces frown. I sometimes hear deep sighs. As an external consultant, I understand that accountability and holding leaders accountable is probably one of the most challenging parts of equity work. It's uncomfortable to be called out or criticized for causing harm. So rather than opening up what could be an amazing opportunity for growth, development, and evolution as an individual and an organization, leaders shy away from this critical step. One important thing I hope you take away from this book is that *one of the most instrumental ways to decenter whiteness and foster an environment built on equity and inclusion is by having accountability measures in place and actually utilizing them.*

I will admit that although I've worked with a number of organizations and institutions where either I have suggested accountability measures, their employees have suggested them, or we've both suggested them, my suggestions are usually ignored and overlooked and leadership refuses to hold themselves accountable. Many leaders feel like there's no point for them to implement accountability measures. The attitude is: *I am the leader; therefore, I must always be right.* But in the long run, when you hold yourself accountable, you're strengthening your organization and increasing your sustainability. A failure to hold people accountable for the harm they're caused means losing talent and no longer being competitive as an organization. People don't want to work at places where they don't feel valued, where they have to adhere to invisible and impossible white standards. A failure to prioritize accountability measures will leave your workplace in a precarious and vulnerable position and inhibit growth.

Employee Feedback

As mentioned throughout this book, employee feedback is the best way to understand how whiteness is being centered in your workplace. Employee feedback can also be instrumental in helping you to be accountable for decentering whiteness. Now that you're almost at the end of this book, you may feel invigorated and empowered to change your workplace culture. But after you've forgotten the words you've read on these pages, who or what will actually hold you responsible for the action items you were planning as you were reading? Think about ways to gauge employee sentiments. I've suggested that some leaders use a questionnaire tool that allows employees (and perhaps even customers) to rate the culture of equity the organization is cultivating. Just as you evaluate employee performance, employees should be able to assess and evaluate the workplace culture and their leaders specifically. If I know that I'll be evaluated every quarter by my direct reports, I'll be more mindful of the culture I'm creating on my team.

One way to introduce more employee feedback into your workplace process is to include it as a part of manager and leader evaluation systems. Managers are often evaluated based on factors like their team's performance, their communication skills, and whether they're able to manage the team effectively. An additional criterion could be equity skills, or the culture of equity that a manager is cultivating on the team.

You can assess this by asking employees questions like "Do you feel like your manager values your contributions on the team?" and "Do you feel like you're treated fairly on the team?" Employees can answer these and other questions on a five-point Likert scale, where they rate the extent to which they agree or disagree with the statement. The employee evaluation could also be a qualitative survey where employees write brief statements about their experiences. For larger organizations that have the resources, I think both a quantitative and qualitative manager evaluation system is best. For smaller organizations, nonprofits, and workplaces without a lot of resources, a qualitative assessment where employees are writing in their feedback may be easier to address and evaluate.

Leadership Accountability

What can be done to incentivize leadership to move toward decentering whiteness? Some companies have seen success with giving monetary rewards for leaders that help them achieve diversity metrics. I don't know if I'm the hugest fan of this approach. Although the carrot/stick model may help your workplace increase racial diversity, if you're inviting employees into a harmful and toxic environment, more issues will arise. Also, hiring employees just to be seen as a "diverse" workplace is tokenizing.

Employee feedback is a powerful way to hold leaders accountable. What will be done to address leaders who are engaging in continuous and ongoing harm? Get really clear on what actions will be taken for leaders engaging in harmful behaviors. Consider if these leaders are "high performers"; sometimes organizations continue to employ toxic, harmful, racist leaders because they're generating a lot of revenue for the company. There must be structures in place to address leaders who are behaving badly. What training and growth opportunities can you provide or are already available for leaders? Every leader should receive coaching and guidance on developing their emotional intelligence and cultivating an equitable environment. Think about how you can incentivize leaders non-monetarily. What reward systems could you create to hold leaders accountable for decentering whiteness in your workplace?

Progress toward Objectives

My clients often forget to share their wins and progress with their workplace. What were the objectives that you were working toward and how far away are you from your target? I understand that the diversity targets are much easier to measure because if they're related to race, ethnicity, and gender, those are visible characteristics that are easier to assess. Objectives like inclusion, equity, and belonging are much more complicated to assess. As you're thinking about specific objectives that you can work toward in your workplace, also consider the metrics that you can use to assess them. Share your journey with everyone internally. Part of the issue I encounter is that there may be progress, although slow, from all these new interventions in the workplace, but on the surface, it may still seem like nothing is being done and nothing has changed. Don't be shy about sharing your goals and objectives for each new year or new quarter and also continuously providing information about progress. Be transparent about setbacks and challenges as well; employees can be instrumental in helping you overcome them.

System Change

In addition to changing policies that are white-centric, how will you modify and reconstruct systems and structures so that whiteness is not central in your workplace? There are many layers to decentering whiteness, and the people in your organization will play an integral part. It isn't as simple as hiring non-white people if there are workplace systems and structures that allow whiteness and white culture to be dominant and centered. How will you change workplace systems so whiteness is decentralized? It will take a combination of policy and systems change, outside support from internal and external equity practitioners, and accountability measures. Many workplaces were founded by known white supremacists; burning these organizations and institutions to the ground may not be realistic or feasible. Sustained system change is needed.

How can system change actually be measured? This is a question I get a lot from leaders. Every workplace is different and, in each industry, what's considered "success" is subjective. The best way to measure system change in your workplace is through your employees, and particularly your most marginalized employees. No matter how much you've invested in DEI programming and education, if employee experiences aren't improving, the system is not successful. There are three areas you can assess to measure whether system change is taking place in your workplace: 1) resignation letters and exit interview data, 2) employee survey data and anonymous channels, and 3) HR reports.

We've discussed resignation letters and exit interview data throughout the book, but I want you to consider some ways to quantify this. How many resignation letters/emails are you receiving each year? How many of those letters mention a particular issue—pay inequity, for example? If one hundred employees have left your organization in the last year and twenty of their resignation letters mentioned pay inequity as an issue, this is a problem. Introduce different measures like pay audits to ensure pay equity and pay transparency. Assess resignation letters again the following year. If the same number of employees are leaving but fewer of them are mentioning pay inequity as an issue, this could be an indication that the situation is improving.

Employee survey data is easier to assess for changes and improvements, especially if it's quantitative data. For smaller organizations or those who haven't been able to integrate employee feedback surveys, assess employee feedback in general. It could be as simple as developing and distributing a Google Form to assess employee sentiments. What feedback are managers receiving from their employees? What feedback is coming through anonymous channels in your workplace? Has the nature or number of employee complaints changed?

Similarly, work with your HR department to evaluate employee reports, write-ups, and other negative workplace experiences that have been reported. For example, is the number of Black employees who are reporting racial inequities declining? This decline may be attributed to several different factors, but if you have the same number of Black employees in your workplace yet the nature of their feedback has improved, this could be a sign you're moving in the right direction. It's important to reiterate that decreases in these types of HR reports and claims could be the result of several different factors (e.g., fear of speaking out or of retaliation). If these types of claims decrease following a particular intervention, it could be because the particular initiative, program, or intervention was effective. Your employees and employee sentiment ultimately determine whether system change has taken place in your workplace and will be the key indicator in your journey toward decentering whiteness.

conclusion

Where Do You Begin?

You now have all the tools you need to decenter whiteness in your workplace. I hope that this book provided you with many insights to both understand the ways that whiteness is centered in your workplace and also recognize tools that you can introduce and implement to decenter whiteness. I will reiterate that change takes time, and that decentering whiteness will not be an easy process. At times, you may feel like giving up.

White-dominant culture is complex and deeply entrenched in all of us. No book can provide you with neat, cookie-cutter solutions to every problem you'll encounter on your journey to decentering whiteness in your workplace. After reading this book, you may feel an urge to run out and try every single intervention that I've suggested. Urgency is an aspect of white culture. I want you to pause for a second. Resist that urge. Yes. You now have many tools to decenter whiteness in your workplace, but what will be your starting point? There is no one-size-fits-all answer. It all depends on what your specific workplace needs are.

This book is not intended to provide you with easy step-by-step instructions and should not be taken as a set-in-stone guide. These are malleable solutions, strategies, and concepts for you to chew on, try out, and refer back to frequently. Our notions of whiteness and the ways that whiteness operates in our systems and structures may change, so please keep in mind that as society evolves, the ways we work to decenter whiteness must evolve as well.

Where do you begin now that you've read this book or the chapters most relevant to you? The first step is to reflect. Let what you've read marinate. What did you learn that you didn't know? Were there any tools mentioned that you were already familiar with, and have you introduced any of the suggested interventions already? It's helpful to revisit each chapter and decide on one specific area of your workplace where you think whiteness is centered the most. For some organizations, it may be in your advancement and promotion process. In other institutions, it could be in your hiring process. In other workplaces, it may be your interview process, and for some of you, it could be a combination of all of these. But choose one area to focus on, and get to work.

Challenges to Decentering Whiteness

Decentering whiteness won't be easy. As with any journey you embark on, you can anticipate challenges along the way. There are three main challenges you may experience when trying to decenter whiteness in your workplace. The first is what you will experience internally. Any time we change habits and develop new patterns, our minds and bodies fight back and want to revert to old ways. But the beautiful thing about humans is that we are so adaptable.

As I've mentioned, years ago I used to compete as an amateur body-builder. One habit I picked up through bodybuilding that I still do now is drinking a gallon of water every day. Sometimes people are amazed by this. I remember a friend asking me, "Don't you wake up in the middle of the night to pee a lot?" At first, I did. It was definitely an adjustment. But over time, my body started getting used to it and I adapted. Now it's to the point where if I *don't* drink my one gallon, I feel excessively thirsty and dehydrated. We are intelligent beings, and although the pull of our old habits is strong, we can overcome them and relearn new habits.

Centering whiteness is something we've all learned to do since birth. The decades we've spent centering whiteness will take constant time, effort, and energy to decenter. Even as I'm writing this book, I know that there are ways I still center whiteness in my life, and I'm actively working to overcome that. At first, you may feel like you're constantly at war with yourself, deviating from your natural inclinations. When I look in the mirror, for example, and see my natural 4c hair, it has taken a reprogramming (that I still work on daily) to resist the urge to see my hair as ugly. Affirmations help me a lot, perhaps because I am a words-of-affirmation person. Speaking verbal affirmations internally or aloud is a reminder that helps me actively decenter whiteness in my own life. It's vital to reframe our white-centered self-talk with more affirming language about the parts of ourselves that white supremacy culture has taught us to hate.

If you're a white person reading this, you have the ability to use your power to influence more spaces than your non-white counterparts do. The second challenge you may experience on your journey to decentering whiteness is the pushback from others in your workplace. It is hard to decenter whiteness if you don't recognize the ways that whiteness is so central. Use your power for good, and push back in any ways that you can in your workplace. Invite your friends, family, coworkers, and leaders to read this book and strategize on which interventions you want to focus on implementing first. White folks reading this book may feel angry and upset at the idea that whiteness must be decentered. You may even feel like this is a personal affront to who you are—trust me, it's not. White-dominant culture is harming us all. The sooner we begin to decenter whiteness in our lives, the sooner we can start creating a better world.

The third challenge you may experience on this decentering whiteness journey is from society at large. For those of your reading this book who are Black, Indigenous, South Asian, East Asian, Pacific Islander, Middle Eastern/North African, or from any other non-white group, do not be deterred by the pushback you'll inevitably experience as you work to decenter whiteness. Florida governor Ron DeSantis is actively defunding DEI initiatives across the state,[1] and the College Board has announced that it has revamped (read: stripped down) its Advanced Placement course in African American studies following backlash from DeSantis and other conservatives.[2] I imagine that this is only the beginning. I anticipate pushback for writing this book. I anticipate disparaging and denigrating remarks and emails. Maybe there will even be some book bans. But that just lets me know that I'm pushing the right buttons and have put something out into the world that needs to be read. We often feel uncomfortable when we are in the midst of growth. Don't be deterred by the resistance you may experience in your workplace.

You picked this book up for a reason. I'm glad the title or some aspect of this book piqued your interest. I truly believe the cliché that everything happens for a reason. You didn't get this book by happenstance. Remember: whiteness has been our way of life for so long that this will be a challenging transition at first. But over time, it will get easier. Keep pushing. Mobilize and strategize with others. Start book clubs and communities around decentering whiteness. This is important and necessary work. Whiteness is the air that we breathe and the water that we drink. Divorcing ourselves from it will be a meandering and challenging but fulfilling journey. There will be no overnight miracles, but to put a spin on one of my favorite quotes from author Reni Eddo-Lodge, every voice that pushes back against whiteness chips away at its power.[3]

decentering whiteness in the workplace discussion guide

I hope that reading *Decentering Whiteness in the Workplace* was informative and provided you with new insights to address racism and understand how whiteness is centered in your workplace. Consider these important discussion questions from each chapter as you begin your journey to decentering whiteness in both your workplace and your personal life.

CHAPTER 1

1. At what point in your life did you start to understand what whiteness was?

2. What factors have shaped your conception and understanding of whiteness?

CHAPTER 2

1. How is whiteness centered in your job postings?

    a. What are ways you can begin to decenter whiteness in your job postings?

2. Do you use an applicant tracking system (ATS) in your hiring process?

    a. How is whiteness prioritized in your ATS?

3. How is whiteness centered in your hiring committees?

    a. How can you actively work to decenter whiteness within your hiring committees?

4. How is whiteness centered when evaluating job candidates?

   a. How can you decenter whiteness when evaluating job candidates?

5. How is whiteness centered in your job interviews?

   a. In what ways can you decenter whiteness in your job interview process?

6. In what ways does your referral hiring program center whiteness?

   a. If you want to continue using a referral hiring program, how can you decenter whiteness in this program?

CHAPTER 3

1. How do you center whiteness when evaluating employee performance?

   a. What strategies can you utilize to decenter whiteness in your performance evaluation process?

2. In what ways does your advancement and promotion process center whiteness?

   a. How can you decenter whiteness in your advancement and promotion process?

3. In what ways is whiteness centered in your customer service practices?

   a. How can you decenter whiteness in your customer service practices?

CHAPTER 4

1. Which of your workplace policies center whiteness?

   a. How will you work to decenter whiteness in your workplace policies?

2. Do any of your customer service policies center and prioritize only white customers?

   a. How can you work to decenter whiteness in your customer service policies?

3. How are your appearance policies white-centric?

   a. How can you decenter whiteness in your appearance policies?

4. In what ways are your standards of professionalism in the work-place white-centered?

   a. How you will work to decenter whiteness in your standards of professionalism?

5. How is your bereavement leave policy white-centered?

   a. How will you decenter whiteness in your bereavement policy?

6. In what ways are your employee work arrangements white-centric?

   a. How can you decenter whiteness in your employee work arrangements?

CHAPTER 5

1. Which voices are centered in your workplace?

2. In what ways are white voices centered in your workplace?

   a. How will you decenter white voices in your workplace?

3. How are white voices centered during your team meetings?

   a. How can you actively decenter white voices during your team meetings?

4. In what ways are the experiences of your white employees centered?

   a. Has there been evidence of tone policing and racial gaslighting in your workplace?

b. What steps can you take to prevent these behaviors from happening?

c. What steps can you take to address these behaviors when/if they occur?

5. What data do you collect about employee experiences?

a. How is that data white-centered?

b. How will you start the process to decenter the whiteness in your employee data?

CHAPTER 6

1. How is whiteness centered in your DEI work?

2. Who engages in your DEI work?

a. How is whiteness centered within your HR department?

b. How is whiteness centered within your DEI team?

c. In what ways can your chief diversity officer, your HR department, and your DEI team actively decenter whiteness?

3. In what ways do you center white comfort in your workplace?

4. Do you engage with external DEI practitioners?

a. In what ways are they actively decentering whiteness in their work?

5. What processes do you utilize to source vendors and independent contractors?

a. How is whiteness centered in that process?

CHAPTER 7

1. Is empathy-building part of your DEI and anti-racism strategy?

2. In what ways is your ability to empathize with others white-centered?

3. What opportunities can you provide employees with to strengthen their compassionate listening skills and practice the three Rs (listen without feeling the need to respond, relate, or recommend)?

CHAPTER 8

1. In what ways have you centered whiteness throughout your life?

2. Who or what taught you to center whiteness?

3. What steps can you actively take to decenter whiteness in your own life?

   a. For those who are non-white: What stereotypes about your racial/ethnic/cultural group have you internalized?

   b. For those who are white: What stereotypes about other racial/ethnic/cultural groups have you heard from friends, family, or community members?

4. What content can you consume to actively decenter whiteness in your life?

5. Do you belong to any communities that can help you to decenter whiteness in your life?

6. What strategies can you utilize to strengthen your humility?

CHAPTER 9

1. What specific feedback have you received from your non-white employees?

   a. How can you collect qualitative data from your employees?

   b. Are you disaggregating employee data and feedback to assess for racial differences?

2. In what ways can you center your marginalized employees?

3. In what ways do your workplace DEI efforts require more specificity?

4. What tailored interventions can you create for employees from racially marginalized backgrounds?

5. What education can you introduce to center your employees from racially marginalized communities?

    a. What topics can you focus your learning and development around?

6. What safe spaces do you have for employees from racially marginalized backgrounds?

CHAPTER 10

1. In what ways do you center Black employees in your workplace?

2. In what ways can you educate employees about the Black community?

3. What are the specific needs of your Black employees?

CHAPTER 11

1. What are the specific actions you will take after reading this book?

    a. Write down three specific actions.

2. Out of the three steps (awareness, acknowledgment and acceptance, accountability), which step of decentering whiteness are you currently in?

    a. What strategies can you use to increase employee awareness?

    b. What sorts of acknowledgments can you make regarding past workplace harms?

    c. What sorts of accountability systems can you implement into your workplace?

3. What barriers and challenges do you anticipate when it comes to decentering whiteness in your workplace?

    a. How will you overcome these barriers and challenges?

4. Which other employees are committed to decentering whiteness in the workplace?

5. In what ways can you stay accountable for decentering whiteness in the workplace?

notes

Introduction

1. "White supremacy," *Merriam-Webster* Online, accessed April 8, 2023, https://www.merriam-webster.com/dictionary/white%20supremacy.
2. Janice Gassam Asare, "4 Ways White Supremacy Harms Humanity," *Forbes*, May 23, 2022, https://www.forbes.com/sites/janicegassam/2022/05/21/4-ways-white-supremacy-harms-humanity/?sh=1f5164926312.
3. Janice Gassam Asare, "4 Ways That White Supremacy Harms White People," *Forbes*, December 10, 2021, https://www.forbes.com/sites/janicegassam/2020/09/18/4-ways-that-white-supremacy-harms-white-people/?sh=74b1a1e8199e.

Chapter 1

1. Angela Y. Davis, *Freedom Is a Constant Struggle: Ferguson, Palestine, and the Foundations of a Movement* (Chicago: Haymarket Books, 2016).
2. Theodore W. Allen, *The Invention of the White Race: The Origin of Racial Oppression* (New York: Verso, 2022), 239.
3. Nell Irvin Painter, *The History of White People* (New York: W. W. Norton & Company, 2010), xi.
4. Painter, *History*, 201.
5. Painter, *History*, 293.
6. Painter, *History*, 134.
7. Painter, *History*, 206.
8. Karen Brodkin, *How Jews Became White Folks and What That Says About Race in America* (New Brunswick, NJ: Rutgers University Press, 2010), 103.
9. Noel Ignatiev, *How the Irish Became White* (New York: Routledge, 2009), 42.
10. Ignatiev, *Irish*, 49.
11. Ignatiev, *Irish*, 113–115.

12. Ignatiev, *Irish*, 130.

13. Suge Knight (@meccavellii), "Like the lasr [*sic*] 3-4 weeks has been weird to watch ! Pls stop!," November 4, 2022, TikTok, https://www.tiktok.com/@meccavellii/video/7162310331862158634?.

14. William H. Frey, "The US Will Become 'Minority White' in 2045, Census Projects," Brookings, March 9, 2022, https://www.brookings.edu/blog/the-avenue/2018/03/14/the-us-will-become-minority-white-in-2045-census-projects/.

15. Brodkin, *Jews*, 70.

16. Brodkin, *Jews*, 71.

17. Janice Z. Gassam Asare, *The Pink Elephant: A Practical Guide to Creating an Anti-Racist Organization* (New York: BWG Business Solutions, 2020).

18. US Census Bureau, "About the Topic of Race," Census.gov, March 1 2022, https://www.census.gov/topics/population/race/about.html.

Chapter 2

1. Danielle Gaucher et al. "Evidence That Gendered Wording in Job Advertisements Exists and Sustains Gender Inequality," *Journal of Personality and Social Psychology* 101, no. 1 (2011): 109–28, https://doi.org/10.1037/a0022530.

2. Madison Feller, "'I Never Thought a Company Would Go This Far': Carla Barrientos on Suing A&F for Racial Discrimination," *ELLE*, April 20, 2022, https://www.elle.com/culture/movies-tv/a39764832/abercrombie-and-fitch-discrimination-lawsuit-details-white-hot/.

3. Benoit Denizet-Lewis, "The Man behind Abercrombie & Fitch," *Salon*, January 24, 2006, https://www.salon.com/2006/01/24/jeffries/.

4. Amy Mackelden, "Netflix's 'White Hot' and the Complicated History of Abercrombie & Fitch," *Harper's BAZAAR*, April 20, 2022, https://www.harpersbazaar.com/culture/film-tv/a39736086/who-is-mike-jeffries-abercrombie-and-fitch-netflix-white-hot/.

5. Heather Barbour Wyatt, "7 Examples of Racial Bias in Job Descriptions," Ongig, August 5, 2020, https://blog.ongig.com/diversity-and-inclusion/racial-bias-in-job-descriptions/.

6. Scottie Andrew and Harmeet Kaur, "Everyday Words and Phrases That Have Racist Connotations," CNN, July 7, 2020, https://www.cnn.com/2020/07/06/us/racism-words-phrases-slavery-trnd/index.html.

7. "70 Inclusive Language Principles That Will Make You a More Successful Recruiter," Handshake, accessed February 14, 2023, https://joinhandshake.com/blog/employers/70-inclusive-language-principles-that-will-make-you-a-more-successful-recruiter/.

8. Phillip R., "Bias Guidance for Inclusive Job Descriptions." Datapeople, accessed January 5, 2023, https://datapeople.io/article/bias-guidance-for-inclusive-job-descriptions/.

9. James Hu, "Report: 99% of Fortune 500 Companies Use Applicant Tracking Systems." Jobscan, November 7, 2019, https://www.jobscan.co/blog/99-percent -fortune-500-ats/.

10. "What Is an Applicant Tracking System?" Oracle, accessed April 6, 2023, https://www.oracle.com/human-capital-management/recruiting/what-is -applicant-tracking-system/#link6.

11. Ashley Nellis, PhD, "The Color of Justice: Racial and Ethnic Disparity in State Prisons," Sentencing Project, October 13, 2021, https://www.sentencingproject. org/reports/the-color-of-justice-racial-and-ethnic-disparity-in-state-prisons -the-sentencing-project/.

12. Daniel Widner and Stephen Chicoine, "It's All in the Name: Employment Discrimination against Arab Americans," *Sociological Forum* 26, no. 4 (2011): 806–23, https://doi.org/10.1111/j.1573-7861.2011.01285.x.

13. Jens Agerström et al., "Warm and Competent Hassan = Cold and Incompetent Eric: A Harsh Equation of Real-Life Hiring Discrimination," *Basic and Applied Social Psychology* 34, no. 4 (2012): 359–66, https://doi.org/10.1080/01973533 .2012.693438.

14. Erez Levon, Devyani Sharma, and Christian Ilbury, *Speaking Up: Accents and Social Mobility* (London: Sutton Trust, 2022), https://www.suttontrust.com/wp -content/uploads/2022/11/Accents-and-social-mobility.pdf.

15. Friedrich-Schiller-Universität Jena, "Psychologists Show How Accent Shapes Our Perception of a Person," ScienceDaily, December 20, 2010, www.science daily.com/releases/2010/12/101217145649.htm.

16. Christine Ro, "The Pervasive Problem of 'Linguistic Racism,'" BBC, June 3, 2021, https://bbc.in/3zzUM5p.

17. Emily Flitter, "At Wells Fargo, a Quest to Increase Diversity Leads to Fake Job Interviews," *New York Times*, May 19, 2022, https://nyti.ms/40NmqYm.

18. Madeline Coleman, "Flores: Broncos Held 'Sham' Interview to Suffice Rooney Rule," *Sports Illustrated*, February 1, 2022, https://www.si.com/nfl/2022/02/01 /brian-flores-broncos-sham-interview-rooney-rule.

Chapter 3

1. Michael Lipka, "A Closer Look at Jehovah's Witnesses Living in the U.S.," Pew Research Center, April 26, 2016, https://pewrsr.ch/2YJACFh.

2. PRRI Staff, "The 2020 Census of American Religion," PRRI, July 8 2021, https:// www.prri.org/research/2020-census-of-american-religion/.

3. Robert R. McCrae and Oliver P. John, "An Introduction to the Five-Factor Model and Its Applications," *Journal of Personality* 60, no. 2 (1992): 175–215, https://doi.org/10.1111/j.1467-6494.1992.tb00970.x.

4. Quinisha Jackson-Wright, "To Promote Inclusivity, Stay Away from Personality Assessments," *New York Times*, August 22, 2019, https://nyti.ms/2Zird3L.

5. Keith J. Caldwell, "Racial Bias and Student Ratings of Instructors," University of Pittsburgh Center for Teaching and Learning, Office of Measurement and Evaluation of Teaching (OMET), accessed April 7, 2023, https://teaching.pitt.edu /resources/racial-bias-and-student-ratings-of-instructors/.

6. Devin G. Pope, Joseph Price, and Justin Wolfers, "Awareness Reduces Racial Bias," National Bureau of Economic Research (NBER) working paper 19765, December 2013, http://www.nber.org/papers/w19765.

7. Lyssa Test, "Performance Review Calibrations: What You Need to Know," Culture Amp, accessed September 19, 2022, https://www.cultureamp.com/blog /performance-review-calibrations.

8. Bryan Hancock et al., "Race in the Workplace: The Black Experience in the US Private Sector," McKinsey & Company, February 21, 2021, https://mck.co/3GtxB0u.

9. Janice Gassam Asare, "Overcoming the Angry Black Woman Stereotype," *Forbes*, May 31, 2019, https://www.forbes.com/sites/janicegassam/2019/05/31 /overcoming-the-angry-black-woman-stereotype/?sh=2a9c5c631fce.

10. Lynnette Khalfani-Cox, "Here's What the 'Black Tax' Does to So Many Families— Including Mine," Vox, March 15, 2021, https://www.vox.com/the-highlight /22323477/personal-finance-black-tax-racial-wealth-gap.

11. Lola Okolosie, "SheaMoisture Is Just the Latest Brand to Erase Black Women from Our Own Picture," *Guardian*, April 27, 2017, https://www.theguardian. com/commentisfree/2017/apr/27/brands-black-women-hair-sheamoisture.

12. Lauren Stewart, "Amid TikTok Controversy, Mielle Organics Joins Procter & Gamble Beauty," NBC Chicago, January 19, 2023, https://www.nbcchicago. com/news/local/amid-tiktok-controversy-mielle-organics-joins-procter -gamble-beauty/3045100/.

Chapter 4

1. Indeed Editorial Team, "16 Examples of Important Workplace Policies," Indeed, last updated March 10, 2023, https://www.indeed.com/career-advice/career -development/workplace-policy-examples.

2. Yon Pomrenze and Darran Simon, "Black Men Arrested at Philadelphia Starbucks Reach Agreements," CNN, May 3, 2018, https://cnn.it/3MmM7ea.

3. Leah Goodridge, "Professionalism as a Racial Construct," *UCLA Law Review*, March 30, 2022, https://www.uclalawreview.org/professionalism-as-a-racial -construct/.

4. Adam Liptak, "Muslim Woman Denied Job over Head Scarf Wins in Supreme Court," *New York Times*, June 1, 2015, https://nyti.ms/2FXQx5B.

5. Chrissy Callahan, "News Anchor Says She Was Fired for Her 'Unprofessional' Natural Hairstyle," TODAY, January 17, 2019, https://www.today.com/style /brittany-noble-was-told-her-natural-hair-was-unprofessional-fired-t146857.

6. Tamar Lewin, "Beard Ban Ruled Unfair to Blacks," *New York Times*, November 3, 1993, https://nyti.ms/3ZSWYzm.

7. Daryl A. Norwood et al., "Pseudofolliculitis Barbae: Prevention and Treatment," *U.S. Pharmacist* 41, no. 10 (2016): 37–40, https://www.uspharmacist.com/article /pseudofolliculitis-barbae-prevention-and-treatment.

8. Janice Gassam Asare, "How One Viral LinkedIn Post Exposed the Need for More Inclusive HR Policies," *Forbes*, September 19, 2021, https://www.forbes.com/sites/janicegassam/2021/09/18/how-one-viral-linkedin-post-exposed -the-need-for-more-inclusive-hr-policies/?sh=765947e855e1.

9. "Operation Definition," APA Dictionary of Psychology, accessed April 8, 2023, https://dictionary.apa.org/operational-definition.

10. "President Biden's State of the Union Address," WhiteHouse.gov, March 1, 2022, https://www.whitehouse.gov/state-of-the-union-2022/.

11. James Gordon, "Malcolm Gladwell Slams Employees Who Work from Home Saying the Concept Is 'Hurting Society,'" *Daily Mail*, August 7, 2022, https:// www.dailymail.co.uk/news/article-11086337/Malcolm-Gladwell-slams -employees-work-home-saying-concept-hurting-society.html.

12. Sheela Subramanian, "A New Era of Workplace Inclusion: Moving from Retrofit to Redesign," Future Forum, March 11, 2021, https://futureforum.com/2021/03 /11/dismantling-the-office-moving-from-retrofit-to-redesign/.

Chapter 5

1. Kelly Gilmore, "Chris Rock Says Will Smith Has 'Selective Outrage' with Oscars Slap during Netflix Comedy Special," E! Online, March 5, 2023, https://eonli.ne /3UoFTMH.

2. New York University, "Psychologists Find Unintentional Racial Biases May Affect Economic and Trust Decisions," ScienceDaily, April 26, 2011, www .sciencedaily.com/releases/2011/04/110425153551.htm.

3. David Yi, "As an Asian American, I Am Invisible in This Country," HuffPost, November 14, 2016, https://www.huffpost.com/entry/as-an-asian-american -i-am-invisible-in-this-country_b_582a019be4b02b1f5257a6f8.

4. Shelby Billups et al., "On Intersectionality: Visualizing the Invisibility of Black Women," *Cognitive Research: Principles and Implications* 7, no. 100 (2022), https://doi.org/10.1186/s41235-022-00450-1.

5. Stephanie Saul, "Despite Years of Criticism, the U.S. News College Rankings Live On," *New York Times*, September 15, 2022, https://nyti.ms/400qZxC.

6. Janice Gassam Asare, "Have We Been Wrongfully Vilifying DEI Training?" *Forbes*, October 7, 2022, https://www.forbes.com/sites/janicegassam /2022/10/07/have-we-been-wrongfully-vilifying-dei-training/?sh =50584b383b35.

7. Janice Z. Gassam Asare, *The Pink Elephant: A Practical Guide to Creating an Anti-Racist Organization* (New York: BWG Business Solutions, 2020).

8. Amanda Shendruk, "Are You Even Trying to Stop Racism If You Don't Collect Data on Race?," Quartz, July 8, 2021, https://qz.com/2029525/the-20-countries-that-dont-collect-racial-and-ethnic-census-data.

Chapter 6

1. "Chief Diversity Officer Demographics and Statistics [2023]: Number of Chief Diversity Officers in the US," Zippia, accessed September 9, 2022, https://www.zippia.com/chief-diversity-officer-jobs/demographics/.

2. Rebekah Bastian, "Black Founders Are Missing Out on Venture Funding for Diversity Hiring Platforms," *Forbes*, September 17, 2021, https://www.forbes.com/sites/rebekahbastian/2021/09/17/black-founders-are-missing-out-on-venture-funding-for-diversity-hiring-platforms/?sh=19d70d892b98.

3. Kirk Johnson, Richard Pérez-Peña, and John Eligon, "Rachel Dolezal, in Center of Storm, Is Defiant: 'I Identify as Black,'" *New York Times*, June 16, 2015, https://nyti.ms/3nVk5Mz.

4. Colleen Flaherty, "Prominent Scholar Outs Herself as White Just as She Faced Exposure for Claiming to Be Black," *Inside Higher Ed*, September 4, 2020, https://www.insidehighered.com/news/2020/09/04/prominent-scholar-outs-herself-white-just-she-faced-exposure-claiming-be-black.

5. David Oliver, "Raquel Evita Saraswati, Rachel Dolezal and the Scandal of Pretending to Be Another Race," *USA Today*, March 2, 2023, https://www.usatoday.com/story/life/health-wellness/2023/03/02/rachel-dolezal-raquel-evita-saraswati-pretending-race/11323159002/.

6. Janice Gassam Asare, "Trump Bans Diversity Training, Claiming It's Divisive, Anti-American Propaganda," *Forbes*, September 5, 2020, https://www.forbes.com/sites/janicegassam/2020/09/05/trump-bans-diversity-training-claiming-its-divisive-anti-american-propaganda/?sh=20c4938765ce.

7. Carol Anderson, *White Rage: The Unspoken Truth of Our Racial Divide* (New York: Bloomsbury, 2016).

8. Minda Harts, *The Memo: What Women of Color Need to Know to Secure a Seat at the Table* (New York: SEAL, 2019).

9. "Black Owned DEI Companies + Consultants Currently Accepting New Corporate Clients!!!," https://docs.google.com/spreadsheets/d/1giDIGTd5XvuCrP9n-Y70_NQPegvmcejdg8x3ypM5Iu4/edit#gid=0.

Chapter 7

1. "Empathy," *Merriam-Webster* Online, accessed April 8, 2023, https://www.merriam-webster.com/dictionary/empathy.

2. Janice Gassam Asare, "*Merriam-Webster* Is Changing the Definition of Racism to Reflect Systemic Oppression," *Forbes*, June 11, 2020, https://www.forbes.com /sites/janicegassam/2020/06/11/merriam-webster-is-changing-the-definition -of-racism-to-reflect-systemic-oppression/?sh=77ce8547400f.

3. Janice Gassam Asare, "Empathy: The Key to a Diverse and Inclusive Workplace," *Forbes*, September 25, 2018, https://www.forbes.com/sites/janicegassam/2018/09 /25/empathy-the-key-to-a-diverse-and-inclusive-workplace/?sh=2e24ce187097.

4. Anjuli Sastry and Karen Grigsby Bates, "When LA Erupted in Anger: A Look Back at the Rodney King Riots," NPR, April 26, 2017, https://n.pr/2o2Ho58.

5. "This Day in History: Eric Garner Dies in NYPD Chokehold," History.com, July 15, 2020, https://www.history.com/this-day-in-history/eric-garner-dies -nypd-chokehold.

6. Paul Bloom, *Against Empathy: The Case for Rational Compassion* (New York: Vintage, 2018).

7. Adriana Miranda, "Missing White Woman Syndrome," University of Missouri Kansas City Women's Center, November 29, 2021, https://info.umkc.edu /womenc/2021/11/29/missing-white-woman-syndrome/.

8. "Say Her Name," African American Policy Forum, accessed April 8, 2023, https://www.aapf.org/sayhername.

9. Michael Ray, "Sandy Hook Elementary School Shooting," Britannica, last updated March 29, 2023, https://www.britannica.com/event/Sandy-Hook -Elementary-School-shooting.

10. Janice Gassam Asare, "Does Resharing Past Experiences with Racism Lead to Systemic Changes? Probably Not," *Forbes*, November 28, 2021, https://www .forbes.com/sites/janicegassam/2021/11/28/does-resharing-past-experiences -with-racism-lead-to-systemic-changes-probably-not/?sh=619dc3ee741c.

Chapter 8

1. Carly Stern, "Why BMI Is a Flawed Health Standard, Especially for People of Color," *Washington Post*, May 4, 2021, https://wapo.st/3KTp8q5.

2. Jasmine Gomez, "Here's How Hyperpigmentation Affects Black Skin, According to Dermatologists," *Women's Health*, June 21, 2021, https://www.womens healthmag.com/beauty/a36124259/hyperpigmentation-on-black-skin/.

3. Janice Gassam Asare, "4C Hair Discrimination: An Exploration of Texturism," *Forbes*, July 24, 2022, https://www.forbes.com/sites/janicegassam/2022/07 /24/4c-hair-discrimination-an-exploration-of-texturism-and-how-it-impacts -those-affected/?sh=4216a5e47cae.

4. Janice Gassam Asare, "The Pervasiveness of Racism and Bias in the Media," *Forbes*, April 14, 2022, https://www.forbes.com/sites/janicegassam/2022/02/28 /the-pervasiveness-of-racism-and-bias-in-the-media/?sh=66544b602cc4.

Chapter 9

1. "The Curb-Cut Effect." PolicyLink, accessed April 8, 2023, https://www .policylink.org/resources-tools/curb-cut-effect.

2. "Curb Cut," Builder-Questions.com, accessed April 8, 2023, https://www .builder-questions.com/construction-glossary/curb-cut/.

3. Angela Glover Blackwell, "The Curb-Cut Effect," *Stanford Social Innovation Review* 15, no. 1 (2016): 28–33, https://doi.org/10.48558/YVMS-CC96.

4. Amira Barger, "No, You Are Not 'Over-Indexing on Black,'" PR Daily, August 10, 2022, https://www.prdaily.com/no-you-are-not-over-indexing-on-black/.

5. Tony Bond, "Belonging in the Workplace: What Does It Mean and Why Does It Matter?," Great Place to Work, June 16, 2022, https://www.greatplacetowork .com/resources/blog/belonging-in-the-workplace-what-does-it-mean-and -why-does-it-matter.

6. Janet E. Helms and R. T. Carter, "Development of the White Racial Identity Inventory," in *Black and White Racial Identity: Theory, Research, and Practice*, ed. Janet E. Helms (Westport, CT: Greenwood Press, 1990), 67–80.

7. Benjamin Artz, Amanda Goodall, and Andrew J. Oswald, "Research: Women Ask for Raises as Often as Men, but Are Less Likely to Get Them," *Harvard Business Review*, June 25, 2018, https://hbr.org/2018/06/research-women-ask -for-raises-as-often-as-men-but-are-less-likely-to-get-them.

8. Sandy J. Wayne et al., "The Cost of Managing Impressions for Black Employ- ees: An Expectancy Violation Theory Perspective," *Journal of Applied Psychol- ogy* 108, no. 2 (2023): 208–24, https://doi.org/10.1037/apl0001030.

Chapter 10

1. Combahee River Collective, "The Combahee River Collective: A Black Feminist Statement," in *Capitalist Patriarchy and the Case for Socialist Feminism*, ed. Zillah R. Eisenstein (New York, Monthly Review Press, 1978), 362–72.

2. Isabel Wilkerson, *Caste: The Origins of Our Discontents* (New York: Random House, 2020).

3. Janice Gassam Asare, "Does DEI Focus Too Much on Black People?," *Forbes*, November 8, 2022, https://www.forbes.com/sites/janicegassam/2022/09/25 /does-dei-focus-too-much-on-black-people/?sh=65bc9e3f26d9.

4. Janice Z. Gassam Asare, *The Pink Elephant: A Practical Guide to Creating an Anti-Racist Organization* (New York: BWG Business Solutions, 2020).

5. Neelima Vallangi, "India's Forgotten African Tribe," BBC, August 4, 2016, https:// bbc.in/3GtctY8.

6. "Israel and Occupied Palestinian Territories Archives," Amnesty International, accessed April 8, 2023, https://www.amnesty.org/en/location/middle-east -and-north-africa/israel-and-occupied-palestinian-territories/report-israel -and-occupied-palestinian-territories/.

7. Phil Mercer, "Report Outlines Racism toward Aboriginal Australians during Worst Bushfires on Record," Voice of America (VOA) News, April 16, 2022, https://www.voanews.com/a/report-outlines-racism-toward-aboriginal-australians-during-worst-bushfires-on-record/6532315.html.

8. Shereen Marisol Meraji and Justin Richmond, "'Se Que Soy': Amara La Negra Embraces Her Afro-Latinidad," NPR, March 14, 2018, https://n.pr/2srrfse.

9. "Paying a High Price for Skin Bleaching | Africa Renewal." *United Nations*, United Nations, https://www.un.org/africarenewal/magazine/april-2019-july-2019/paying-high-price-skin-bleaching.

10. Erin Blakemore, "The Harsh Reality of Life under Apartheid in South Africa," History.com, April 26, 2019, https://www.history.com/news/apartheid-policies-photos-nelson-mandela.

11. Isis H. Settles, NiCole T. Buchanan, and Kristie Dotson, "Scrutinized but Not Recognized: (In)visibility and Hypervisibility Experiences of Faculty of Color," *Journal of Vocational Behavior* 113 (2019): 62–74, https://doi.org/10.1016/j.jvb.2018.06.003.

12. Rick Rojas, Neelam Bohra, and Eliza Fawcett, "What We Know about Tyre Nichols's Lethal Encounter with Memphis Police," *New York Times*, February 12, 2023, https://nyti.ms/3Mtuv0b.

13. Kweilin Ellingrud et al., "Diversity, Equity and Inclusion Lighthouses 2023," McKinsey & Company, January 13, 2023, https://mck.co/3KLe4v4.

14. Adriele Parker, "Where the Diversity at? The Truth about Who's Really Researching & Writing About DEI," LinkedIn, January 20, 2023, https://www.linkedin.com/posts/adrieleparker_where-the-diversity-at-the-truth-about-whos-activity-7022306364030865408-vT74/.

15. Allaya Cooks-Campbell, "Code-Switching at Work: What It Is and Why You Need to Understand It," BetterUp, March 1, 2022, https://www.betterup.com/blog/code-switching.

16. Victoria M. Massie, "White Women Benefit Most from Affirmative Action—and Are among Its Fiercest Opponents," Vox, May 25, 2016, https://www.vox.com/2016/5/25/11682950/fisher-supreme-court-white-women-affirmative-action.

17. Arthur Delaney and Alissa Scheller, "Who Gets Food Stamps? White People, Mostly," HuffPost, December 7, 2017, https://www.huffpost.com/entry/food-stamp-demographics_n_6771938.

18. Ryan D. King and Brian D. Johnson, "A Punishing Look: Skin Tone and Afrocentric Features in the Halls of Justice," *American Journal of Sociology* 122, no. 1 (2016): 90–124, https://doi.org/10.1086/686941.

19. Lynnette Khalfani-Cox, "Here's What the 'Black Tax' Does to So Many Families—Including Mine," Vox, March 15, 2021, https://www.vox.com/the-highlight/22323477/personal-finance-black-tax-racial-wealth-gap.

20. Gillian B. White, "Black Workers Really Do Need to Be Twice as Good," *Atlantic*, June 27, 2018, https://www.theatlantic.com/business/archive/2015/10/why -black-workers-really-do-need-to-be-twice-as-good/409276/.

21. Janice Gassam Asare, "The Erasure of Black Women's Contributions: From Past to Present," *Forbes*, April 21, 2022, https://www.forbes.com/sites/janicegassam /2021/10/08/the-erasure-of-black-womens-contributions-from-past-to-present/.

22. Janice Gassam Asare, "New Research Shows That Reparation Payments Could Increase Life Expectancy of Black Americans," *Forbes*, December 1 2022, https:// www.forbes.com/sites/janicegassam/2022/11/29/new-research-shows-that -reparation-payments-could-increase-life-expectancy-of-black-americans /?sh=7ad46cab6a63.

23. Anisa Purbasari Horton, "Sleep Is Critical for Productivity, but Many Still Aren't Getting Enough," Fast Company, November 19, 2019, https://www.fastcompany .com/90429940/surveymonkey-productivity-survey-and-the-racial-sleep-gap.

24. Danielle D. King et al., "Give Black Employees Time to Rest and Recover," *Harvard Business Review*, February 22, 2021, https://hbr.org/2021/02/give-black -employees-time-to-rest-and-recover.

Chapter 11

1. Tre Johnson, "When Black People Are in Pain, White People Just Join Book Clubs," *Washington Post*, June 13, 2020, https://wapo.st/40PRZ47.

2. Harriet A. Washington, "Apology Shines Light on Racial Schism in Medicine," *New York Times*, July 29, 2008, https://nyti.ms/3Kk2G80.

3. "Apology to People of Color for APA's Role in Promoting, Perpetuating, and Failing to Challenge Racism, Racial Discrimination, and Human Hierarchy in U.S.," American Psychological Association, October 29, 2021, https://www.apa.org /about/policy/racism-apology.

4. *Baltimore Sun* Editorial Board, "We Are Deeply and Profoundly Sorry: For Decades, the *Baltimore Sun* Promoted Policies That Oppressed Black Marylanders; We Are Working to Make Amends," *Baltimore Sun*, February 18, 2022, https:// www.baltimoresun.com/opinion/editorial/bs-ed-0220-sun-racial-reckoning -apology-online-20220218-qp32uybk5bgqrcnd732aicrouu-story.html.

5. Rodrigo Pérez Ortega, "Human Geneticists Apologize for Past Involvement in Eugenics, Scientific Racism," *Science*, January 14, 2023, https://www.science .org/content/article/human-geneticists-apologize-past-involvement-eugenics -scientific-racism.

Conclusion

1. Josh Moody, "The New Conservative Playbook on DEI," *Inside Higher Ed*, February 7, 2023, https://www.insidehighered.com/news/2023/02/07/desantis -debuts-new-conservative-playbook-ending-dei.

2. Anemona Hartocollis and Eliza Fawcett, "The College Board Strips Down Its A.P. Curriculum for African American Studies," *New York Times*, February 1, 2023, https://nyti.ms/3nX3TdO.

3. Reni Eddo-Lodge, *Why I'm No Longer Talking to White People about Race* (London: Bloomsbury Publishing, 2019).

acknowledgments

I don't know how to begin to give thanks to all those who have influenced my journey. I must first start by thanking my parents for all the sacrifices they've made to give me a life of opportunity and access. My mom poured so much love into the family and I know I wouldn't be the person I am today without her. To my father, who has influenced me in more ways than I realized: thank you for all that you've done to help me soar.

To my amazing spouse, Michael: your love fuels me. Thank you for your grace, your kindness, and for continuing to motivate and encourage me. Thank you for being a sounding board for me to always bounce my thoughts and ideas off of.

Thank you to my brother and sister, who have influenced me in different ways and have helped me see the world in unique ways.

A huge thanks to all my girls from VCU and those I've connected with post-college. Each of you continues to inspire and motivate me and big me up every chance you get! I couldn't have done this without y'all. The phone calls, group chat conversations, text messages, email messages, and other words of affirmation you have provided me have meant the world to me.

Thank you to Joquina Reed for always being a source of inspiration and for allowing me to bounce ideas off of you. Thank you for sharing your quotes and thoughts for this manuscript and for your sisterhood.

Thank you to Steve Piersanti, for your persistence and all the coaching and guidance you have provided me in this book writing and publishing process! You are the best.

Thank you to the whole Berrett-Koehler team for seeing the value in this book and allowing the world to hear my voice.

index

personality assessments, 34–35
Pew Research Center, 33–34
PhDs, 105, 107
The Pink Elephant, 4–5, 11, 69, 126
"pipeline problem," 27
policies
    appearance, 55–56
    bereavement leave, 56–57
    centering Black employees, 130–141
    centering marginalized groups, 116, 118–123
    customer service, 50–55
    health insurance, 57–58
    to prevent harm, 150–152
    transparency about, 58
    work arrangement, 59–61
    workplace safeguards, 51–54, 123
policing tone, 70
power dynamics, 51, 60
privileges, 9, 72, 79, 83
proactivity, 135
productivity, 35
"professional," 55–56, 58, 84
profit, 51, 52, 60, 80, 87, 88
promotion, 39–44
public acknowledgment, 149
pushback, 161–162

Q

qualitative data, 74, 117, 144–145
quantitative data, 144, 156

R

race
    construct of "white," 8–9
    guesstimates about, 73
    hierarchy of, 9, 10, 125
    Jews as presumed, 9
    lumping together of, 119
    white discomfort with, 107–108
race-fishing, 79
racial classification system, 12
racial gaslighting, 69
racial profiling, 134
Racial Revolution, 149
racism
    attempts to self-shield from, 112
    avoiding discussion of, 83
    at "best of" workplaces, 68
    of college students, 40–41
    and customer service, 36, 134–135
    empathy and, 82, 93

historic racial stigmas, 11–13
invalidation of, 69
recounting traumas of, 94–95
shared language on, 8
variety in felt bias, 119
white experts on, 78
See also systemic racism
rap music, 104–105
reactivity, 135
recruitment, 19–21, 73
Reed, Joquina, 4, 8, 79, 148
referral hiring, 29–31
rejection, humility via, 111
"relate," trying to, 2–3
religion, 10, 33–34, 55
remote work, 59–61
reparations, 139
representation, non-white, 64–65
resignation letters, 145, 156
respectability politics, 104, 105–106
resumes, anonymizing, 21
retention, 42, 73–74, 118
Rock, Chris, 63
Rodriguez, Raven, 138
Rooney Rule, 27
round robin technique, 66
rubric, job, 25–26, 28, 30
Russo-Ukrainian War, 109

S

Saad, Layla, x
Sacco, Tijidankay T.K., 137
safer spaces, 123, 153
safety, employee, 50, 53
salary negotiation, 122
Sandy Hook, 94
Saraswati, Raquel Evita, 80
savior complex, white, 67, 86
Say Her Name, 93
secret shoppers, 36
self-promotion, 122
self-reflection, 77, 108, 135, 160
SheaMoisture, 45
siblings, 56
Siddis, 127
skin color, 78–79, 101
skinniness, 100–102
sleep health, 140
Smith, Will, 63, 64
So You Want to Talk about Race (Oluo), 2
social media

about the author

In 2011, Janice started a YouTube channel focused on her experiences as a Black woman navigating America and her thoughts on racism and Black identity. The channel has since garnered over 4 million views. While she didn't realize it at the time, she was building the blueprint for what would become her work as an anti-racism consultant.

After earning a bachelor's degree in psychology, Janice decided to pursue an MBA from Louisiana State University (LSU). While pursuing both degrees, she worked in banking. Banking piqued her interest in workplace psychology. After a semester and a half at LSU, she realized that she was more interested in learning about how to make workplace dynamics better, and how to improve the overall employee experience. Janice decided to quit her MBA program and pursue a master's degree in industrial organizational psychology instead.

While pursuing that master's degree, Janice pivoted from banking into training and development, where she worked at a local paper mill to help guide train-the-trainer sessions. She decided to continue her schooling and pursue a PhD in applied organizational psychology, which she earned from Hofstra University. During her PhD program, she had the opportunity to start teaching college courses at a local university. Coming from a family of educators, Janice was naturally drawn to the classroom and worked in academia as a professor for seven years before deciding to move into DEI consulting full-time.

In 2018, Janice started BWG Business Solutions, an award-winning DEI consulting firm that focuses on helping workplaces become more equitable. She has had the opportunity to lend her thoughts to *Forbes* as a senior contributing writer, having written nearly four hundred articles on workplace equity that have amassed over 7 million views. Janice now spends her time facilitating workshops and keynote talks on workplace equity for corporate clients, colleges, and universities. She has presented at organizations and institutions like Yale University, Amazon, PayPal/Venmo, Verizon/Yahoo, Salesforce, H&M, New York University, and Nordstrom, among many others.

Janice lives in the New York metropolitan area with her husband, Michael. Prior to New York, she lived in Oman, as well as Minnesota, Virginia, and Louisiana. To learn more about Janice, visit her website, drjanicegassam.com.

Dear reader,

Thank you for picking up this book and welcome to the worldwide BK community! You're joining a special group of people who have come together to create positive change in their lives, organizations, and communities.

What's BK all about?

Our mission is to connect people and ideas to create a world that works for all.

Why? Our communities, organizations, and lives get bogged down by old paradigms of self-interest, exclusion, hierarchy, and privilege. But we believe that can change. That's why we seek the leading experts on these challenges—and share their actionable ideas with you.

A welcome gift

To help you get started, we'd like to offer you a **free copy** of one of our bestselling ebooks:

www.bkconnection.com/welcome

When you claim your **free ebook**, you'll also be subscribed to our blog.

Our freshest insights

Access the best new tools and ideas for leaders at all levels on our blog at ideas.bkconnection.com.

Sincerely,

Your friends at Berrett-Koehler